HOW TO LIVE & WC

In this Series

Other titles in preparation

LIVE & WORK IN ITALY

A handbook for short and long stay visitors

Amanda Hinton

How To Books

British Library Cataloguing-in-publication data
A catalogue record for this book is available from the British Library.

First published in 1993 by How To Books Ltd, Plymbridge House, Estover Road, Plymouth PL6 7PZ, United Kingdom. Tel: Plymouth (0752) 735251/695745. Fax: (0752) 695699. Telex: 45635.

Typeset by Concept Communications (Design & Print) Ltd, Crayford, Kent. Printed and bound by BPCC Wheatons Ltd, Exeter.

Preface

How to Live and Work in Italy has been written for those planning something more than a tourist trip to Italy, and for those who want to do things the Italian way. This means understanding and appreciating Italian lifestyle, learning to live with the idiosyncracies of everyday Italian life, and finding out how to deal with Italian bureaucracy. *How to Live and Work in Italy* should be a useful reference when it comes to making a decision or figuring out how something is done Italian style. It will also give you an insight into Italian life and what makes things tick. Living and working in Italy can be a great experience, as I have found myself during the last few years, and I hope that this book will help you, too, enjoy a very successful stay in this lively country. Good luck!

Amanda Hinton

List of Illustrations

Contents

1
Italy in Brief

INTRODUCING THE COUNTRY

The 'boot' that makes up mainland Italy has its toe in the Mediterranean, the Adriatic on its eastern flank and the Tyrrhenian on the west. The coast, including the islands of Sardinia and Sicily, is 7, 420 km long; mountains make up 35.2 per cent of the country, while gently folding hills cover just over 40 per cent of the rest. All of this makes for a very scenic country, with each region having its own character and landscape.

For purposes of administration Italy is divided into 20 regions: Piedmont, Aosta, Lombardy, Trentino-Alto Adige, Veneto, Friuli-Venezia Giulia, Liguria, Emilia Romagna, Tuscany, Umbria, Marche, Lazio, Abruzzo, Molise, Puglia, Campania, Basilicata, Calabria, Sicily and Sardinia. The regions are further subdivided, and comprise 95 provinces with over 8,000 municipalities, each of which has a strong sense of identity thanks to the Italian's inherent *campanilismo*, parochialism, and sense of local pride.

Pride in all things Italian and a love of life have been little dampened by the onset of economic recession, and Italy continues to be one of the biggest markets for French champagne, Scotch whisky and Rolls Royce cars. Many Italians spend their summer holidays in exotic destinations as well as taking a *settimana bianca* ski holiday during the winter. The close-knit structure of the family helps finance these luxuries as generous old-age pensions are pooled into the household fund.

ITALIAN-STYLE ECONOMICS

On a national scale, however, Italy's finances are in turmoil. It has the third largest budget deficit in the world, amounting to 11 per cent of its total economic output in 1992. Despite this, the underlying economy is fairly robust, particularly when the 'hidden economy' is taken into account. A great many companies are not legally registered and a large

Fig. 1. Map of Italy.

proportion of the labour market is unregulated. For example, Naples is a centre for the production of gloves, yet there is hardly a single registered glove-making company in the city.

Perhaps the greatest drain on the Italian economy has been the mismanagement of funds, with huge sums of money being poured into public construction projects that are rarely completed. The vast and empty aqueducts crossing the parched countryside in the southern regions of Reggio Calabria, and the non-existent housing for earthquake victims, are some of the more poignant examples of funds being intercepted. It's a depressingly commonplace scenario, with fortunes being taken from the industrial north to improve the south, but ending up in the pockets of everyone except the people who need it.

POLITICAL LIFE

Like the economy, the government is also in a state of tumult. For almost 50 years the same people, entrenched in cold-war politics, had been in power, albeit in changed seats. In April 1992, however, the veteran Prime Minister, Giulio Andreotti, who was known for his *immobilismo*, was superceded by Giuliano Amato. Amongst other radical changes, Amato was responsible for introducing an austerity budget in order to bring inflation down to European levels, making sweeping reforms of the welfare state and abolishing the *scala mobili*, the inflationary wage indexation system. The 1990s have also seen the challenging appearance of *leghe*, regional independence movements. At the same time the 1990s have heralded the exposure of Italy's institutional crime. Hundreds of politicians and business men have been arrested for raking off funds into party or personal coffers and billions of dollars of public money have been lost in *tangenti*, kick-backs to secure public contracts. New electoral systems, and a sweeping out of the old faces, coupled with a strengthening of the controls over public funds, look like doing much to overcome this crisis.

Another dramatic turn of the 1990s has been in connection with the Mafia. The savage assassination of the top anti-Mafia investigators, Judge Falcone and his successor Judge Borsellino, sparked a popular revolt in the summer of 1992. For the first time people had the courage to voice opinions that they formerly would not even have dared to think. The Mafia will only be swept away when an honest government once again exerts control, and when the law of silence, the *omertá*, is finally broken.

2
Before You Go

WHAT PAPERWORK WILL I NEED?

UK visitors to Italy need the bare minimum of documents to enter the country. However, Italian bureaucracy with its kilometres of red tape has a way of multiplying the papers needed in any operation, so that in reality you will find that the more documents you can take with you, the better. Obtaining the necessary documents from the UK before travelling to Italy is a wise move, especially if you are intending to become a permanent resident in Italy. If you are making a long-term move try to allow about three months in order to make a thorough job of preparing your papers and tying up all the loose ends before your departure.

Passports and visas

To visit Italy a valid passport, or in the case of EC citizens an identity card, is all that is necessary. British citizens who wish to stay in Italy for more than three months should have a standard ten-year passport rather than the temporary visitor's passport.

Visa requirements for citizens of other countries should be checked at an Italian Consulate (see Appendix for addresses). Should you need a visa you will have to submit an application form and one passport-sized photograph.

Other documents

Once in Italy, those intending to stay for longer than the permitted three months will need to obtain a **Permesso di Soggiorno** (Permit to Stay). It can speed up the procedure if, before leaving the UK, you apply to your nearest Italian Consulate for the appropriate consular stamp or for a letter stating the purpose of your stay. If you intend to register for work in Italy you will need authenticated translations made of your educational or professional qualifications, as well as certificates of equivalence.

Academic and scholastic certificates of equivalence, known as *Certificato di Equipollenza*, are undertaken by the **Ministry of Foreign Affairs** at the following address in Rome:

Ufficio VI
Equipollenze per i paesi Anglofoni
Direzione Generale per le Relazioni Culturali
Ministero degli Affari Esteri
Rome
Tel: (06) 36912701.

Further information on academic recognition can be obtained from the following address:

Centro Informazione sulla Mobilità e le Equivalenze Accademiche
(CIMEA)
Fondazione RUI
Viale XXI Aprile 36
Rome
Tel: (06) 8321281.

If you are not going to work, but intend to live on savings while in Italy, you should obtain a letter from your bank stating your financial position, which can be presented along with your application for a permit.

If you are moving to Italy with your children you should also have authenticated translations made of any educational and vaccination documents they have. To obtain authenticated translations and certificates contact your nearest Italian Consulate well in advance of leaving (see Appendix for Consulate addresses).

Arranging travel insurance

If you intend to take out travel insurance it is best to select a comprehensive policy. This should include medical expenses, personal accident insurance, flight cancellation, personal liability as well as covering personal effects. Remember that if you need to make a claim you will be requested to supply receipts. As this is not always possible, it may be a good idea to have older items, such as jewellery, individually valued and recorded. Keeping a photographic record is not such a bad idea as it offers the insurance company some idea of the objects being claimed for, as well as some proof of their existence.

Health insurance

British citizens, or nationals of other European Community countries who are resident in the UK, are entitled to subsidised medical care under the **Italian State Health Service**. In order to apply, go to a main post office or a social security office and fill in an application form for an **E111**. The E111 is your certificate of entitlement and should be presented when medical care is needed, along with proof of your UK residence. It is advisable to take your NHS card for this purpose, although a passport or driving licence will suffice. You may also be asked to provide a photocopy of your E111, so have a spare copy handy.

It may be worth considering a private health insurance policy which would enable you to opt out of the State Health system, which only provides emergency treatment, doctors and paediatricians free of charge. You will also find that in major cities and in the south of Italy, the State Health system is often overstretched and sub-standard.

● Note that you are only eligible for an E111 if you continue to be a resident of the UK and maintain your National Insurance contributions. Therefore make sure that the DSS Overseas Department (see Appendix for address) is informed of the state of your National Insurance contributions before leaving Britain. You should also remember that an E111 is only valid for one year.

Anyone intending to take up residency in Italy must join the Italian health service (see Chapter Six) or take out a private health insurance policy.

Immunisation

No vaccinations are required to enter Italy.

Social Security

Are you unemployed? Have you been receiving unemployment benefit in Britain for at least four weeks and intend looking for work in Italy? If so you may have your benefit payments transferred for up to three months from the day on which you leave the UK. To be certain that you are eligible read leaflet N112 which is available from the DHSS in the UK. If you are unemployed let the Unemployment Benefit office know well in advance of leaving the country and apply for form E303, which is a certificate of authorisation to look for work in Italy. You should also ask for an introductory letter which is written in Italian (known as Code 2 Appendix L12). This will help you when you register for employment in Italy. If you are registered at a Job Centre in the UK, ask to be registered as a Job Seeker in Italy. Your details will then be forwarded to the Italian Employment Office *(Ufficio Collocamento)*.

If you are receiving Sickness Benefit or Maternity Allowance you should be able to receive payments in Italy until it expires. However, write well in advance to the Department of Social Security Overseas Branch (see Appendix for address) and ask for their authorisation. Ask for pamphlet SA30 which gives further information on receiving Benefit abroad.

If you are receiving a UK Retirement Pension you will continue to receive your payments in Italy. Payments are made either directly by postal orders, or can be deposited in a UK or Italian bank account or building society. Make sure you arrange exactly how the payments are to be paid before leaving.

For further information obtain the DHSS pamphlet SA29, *Your Social Security and Pension Rights in the European Community*.

Students

Students planning to attend an Italian university must go to an Italian Consulate before leaving and obtain a certified declaration stating their acceptance on a course. Students should also make sure that they obtain form E111 (see health insurance above). It is obligatory to present the E111, or a health insurance policy with an Italian Government-assisted company, when applying for a *Permesso di Soggiorno* (Permit to Stay). For further information on applying for a place at an Italian university see Chapter Eight.

Students should also remember to take their student identity card in order to receive discounts on museum entrance fees and travel.

Liability to British tax

Careful consideration needs to be given to the benefits and disadvantages of being either a British or Italian tax payer, or both. The tax laws are numerous and complex in both countries, and constantly change, and it is a good idea to seek professional help on this matter.

However, some general principles are useful to bear in mind. First, Italy and Britain have a **double-taxation agreement** which means that the same income is never taxed in both countries, and that the two tax authorities come to an agreement about who taxes what according to:

● where your principal residence is
● where your income is generated
● and what your nationality is.

Secondly, that exemption from British tax is granted if you are deemed non-resident. To qualify for that status you need to work overseas full time for a year, visit the UK for less than three months a year, have no available accommodation there, nor perform any part of your job there. The exception to this rule is income that derives from property rented out in the UK, which is always liable for UK taxation. If you are planning a short-term stay in Italy you will therefore remain liable to UK income tax, and probably only come up against Italian taxes if you own a property in Italy.

In order to claim non-resident status, obtain Form P85 from either your local Inspector of Taxes or the address below:

Inland Revenue Head Office
Public Departments
Foreign Section
Ty-Glas
Llanishen
Cardiff
Wales CF4 5ZD.

For further information about UK tax apply for leaflet IR20, which is published by the Inland Revenue and is also available either from your local Tax Inspector or from the above address.

Banking

If you are claiming non-resident status in Britain you should inform your bank or building society so that you are exempted from paying tax on any interest that you accrue. You may wish to arrange offshore banking; most of the national banks have offshore branches, which means you can simply transfer your account from one branch to another. It is a good idea to keep a sterling account open as Italian banking is expensive and does not offer the same customer services or facilities. Make sure, however, that you have good access to your sterling account, preferably with an international card that can be used in automatic banking machines at principal Italian banks.

Driving documents

Drivers in Italy will need a current driving licence. If you have an old, green-style UK driving licence, apply for a standard Italian translation, which is free of charge, from the Automobile Association (AA) or the Royal Automobile Club (RAC) (see Appendix for addresses). It is also

available at the frontier offices of Automobile Club Italiano (ACI).
Drivers with the EEC-format licences, which are pink or more recently
pink and green, do not need to carry a translation, nor do drivers with
International Driving Licences. If you hold the latter remember that it is
only valid for one year.

Other documents you should have include:

- **green card insurance**, which is available from your insurance company or at frontier crossing points; the green card is valid for one year
and covers you to drive anywhere in Europe;
- your **V5 Registration Document** (log book);
and a GB sticker, on display.

British-plate vehicles

In European countries you are allowed to drive a foreign vehicle for 12
months. In Italy, however, British-registered vehicles can only be driven
with their original plates for up to six months in any one 12-month period.
Italy also bucks the European norm on importation laws, which is obligatory after six months. It is extraordinarily difficult to import vehicles, and
the authorities may well advise you to continue driving on your original
plates and rely on the police turning a blind eye. The procedure for
importing a vehicle is painstakingly long. You should consider very
carefully whether you really need to import your car into Italy, or whether
it would be better to sell it in the UK before departure and purchase another
upon arrival in Italy, even if car prices are somewhat higher there.

If you are certain you wish to import your vehicle, then read on. Before
leaving Britain complete your V5 Registration document and return it to
DVLC Swansea or your regional Vehicle Registration Office, stating the
date on which you intend to export the vehicle. You should also request
that your V5 Registration Document, or an authenticated photocopy, is
returned along with a **Certificate of Export V561**. Italy is unusual in that
it requests the V5 as well as the V561; normally the V561 replaces the
V5. Once in possession of both these documents you should have them
translated into Italian and authenticated. The Italian authorities also
request a **Scheda Tecnica** which is technical data concerning your
vehicle. This should be available from the head office of the manufac-
turers of your vehicle. Again this needs to be translated and authenticated.
Finally get a copy of the vehicle sales invoice showing the amount of VAT
paid. You may be requested to pay the difference between UK and Italian
VAT when you cross the border into Italy. The next stage in the formalities
takes place in Italy (see Chapter Four).

Tips on car importing
Here are some tips if you are trying to import your vehicle into Italy.

● Cars made outside the EC are almost impossible to import and invoke the payment of very high import taxes.

● To avoid the payment of customs duty and import tax the owner must have owned the vehicle for at least 12 months prior to the date of importation.

● Make sure your V561 certificate of export is stamped when crossing the border into Italy, as this will be proof of the actual date on which you officially imported the vehicle.

● For ease of servicing and parts Renault, Fiat, Volkswagen, Audi, Alfa-Romeo and Mercedes are the most common cars in Italy.

Pets

If you are travelling with a domestic animal you will be asked to present a bilingual **Export Health Certificate** and a **Rabies Certificate** when you enter Italy. To obtain an Export Health Certificate apply to the Ministry of Agriculture, Fisheries and Food at the address below and request application form EXA1.

Ministry of Agriculture, Fisheries and Food Government Buildings
    (Toby Jug Site)
Hook Rise South
Tolworth
Surbiton
Surrey KT6 7NF
Tel: (081) 330 4411.

On receipt of application form EXA1, fill in the necessary information and send it to your local Animal Health Office, which will issue the certificate to an approved Local Veterinary Inspector. The Inspector is responsible for completing the export certificate and examining your animal within 48 hours of your departure.

The rabies vaccine will also be administered by the Local Veterinary Inspector, who will attach the Rabies Certificate to the Export Health Certificate. The rabies vaccine should be given not less than 20 days and not more than 11 months before leaving the UK.

Animals under three months of age, and animals who are being transported unaccompanied, are exempt from the rabies vaccine, although they must undergo an examination by an Italian Veterinary Officer when entering Italy.

If you are travelling through other places on the way to Italy, apply to the authorities in the relevant countries.

CHECKLIST OF DOCUMENTS

Make sure you have the following:

Passport or Identity Card   _____

Form E111 and/or health insurance   _____

NHS card   _____

Travel insurance policy   _____

Student Identity Card   _____

Export Health Certificate (for pets)   _____

Rabies Vaccination Certificate (for pets)   _____

Driving Licence   _____

Translation of Driving Licence   _____

Green card insurance   _____

V5 Registration Document   _____

V561 Certificate of Export   _____

Vehicle sales invoice   _____

WHAT SHOULD I TAKE?

Those planning a short visit to Italy will probably find that everything they require is available there, and need only concern themselves with the customs regulations. Those planning a longer-term trip, or to take up residence in Italy, will find this section helpful as it also suggests what might be taken out to Italy, either because it is not readily available, or because it is considerably more expensive there.

Customs allowances
If you have purchased goods and paid duty and tax within an EC country, your allowance is as follows:

- 300 cigarettes or 75 cigars or 400g of tobacco
- 1.5 litres alcohol with over 22% volume, or
- 3 litres alcohol with under 22% volume, or
- 5 litres table wine
- 1kg coffee or 400g coffee extracts and essences
- 200g tea or 80g tea extracts and essences
- 90cc perfume
- 375cc toilet water
- other goods up to the value of £250.

Duty and tax free shops
If you have purchased goods in a duty- and tax-free shop, your allowance is as follows:

- 200 cigarettes, or 50 cigars, or 250g of tobacco
- 1 litre alcoholic beverage over 22% volume, or
- 2 litres alcoholic beverage under 22% volume, or
- 2 litres table wine
- 500g coffee or 200g coffee extracts and essences
- 100g tea or 40g tea extracts and essences
- 60cc perfume
- 250cc toilet water
- other goods up to the value of £44.

The restrictions on personal effects are supposedly lifted for EC citizens. However, in reality you may be faced with problems when it comes to items such as electrical appliances. If you are moving from Britain to Italy you are likewise free to move your household belongings and personal effects, provided that you have owned them for more than three months and that you paid tax on purchasing them. The only way of proving this is with a sales invoice, so before you leave gather together as many invoices as possible for items you intend to take. If you plan to move your household belongings in stages you will still be exempt from paying tax, provided they are moved within six months of the date you acquired residence in Italy. Exemption from taxes also applies to those moving household effects from Britain to a holiday home in Italy, provided you are the owner of the property or have been paying rent for at least 12 months.

Money

It is a good idea to obtain some Italian lire from the bank before leaving. You are allowed to take up to Lit.20,000,000, or its equivalent in other currencies, either in or out of Italy. If you exceed this allowance you must make a declaration on the V2 form at customs. However, check the currency allowances with your bank at the time of departure as they do fluctuate.

● Notes are issued for Lit.1,000, 2,000, 5,000, 10,000, 50,000 and 100,000, and thanks to inflation at Lit.500,000 too.

● Coins are of Lit.50, 100, 200, 500 and 1,000 denominations.

Furnishings

If you are setting up a home in Italy it is worth considering transporting your furniture from Britain, as it is considerably more expensive in Italy and the cost of replacing household furniture is likely to be higher than the cost of using an international removal firm. There are few secondhand furniture shops in Italy, and old furniture such as pine cupboards and chest of drawers are regarded as antiques and fetch exorbitant prices by British standards.

If you are bringing furniture over 50 years old from Britain you should apply for permission from the Italian Ministry of Culture beforehand, and then declare it on arrival, to avoid difficulties in re-exporting it. The address for the Italian Ministry of Culture is:

Ministero Beni Culturali
Ufficio Esportazione Oggetti d'Arte
Via Cernaia 1
Roma
Tel: (06) 4881457.

If you are planning to decorate your home in Italy you will find DIY materials cheaper and more readily available in Britain. This is especially true of paint, both emulsion and gloss, which are of a far higher quality in the UK, have better ranges of colours and lower prices. It is worth noting that DIY, known as *fai da te*, is in its infancy in Italy. Very few people do their own work, and DIY kits such as flat-pack units or self-assembly articles like roller blinds are not generally available. As Italians take their kitchens with them when they move house you are more than likely to have to put in a new one when buying a property. Great savings can be made by bringing out a complete flat-pack kitchen from the UK, as Italian kitchens, while very attractive, are also very expensive.

Floor coverings are also something you may wish to consider bringing from Britain. Italian homes generally have tiled floors; fitted carpets are not very common and you pay a lot for what seems, by comparison to UK standards, poor quality carpeting.

Bedding in Italy consists mainly of blankets and eiderdowns. If you prefer to sleep under a duvet it is a good thing to bring, as although they are available in some places they are very much more expensive than in the UK.

Electrical appliances
Electrical appliances in Italy run on 220v. In general, it is slightly more expensive to buy electrical appliances in Italy, but on the whole it is more convenient as they are covered by local guarantee and can be repaired easily. Something you are well advised to bring with you, however, is an electric kettle, as they are hard to come by and very expensive in Italy.

If you are bringing electrical appliances from Britain bring the sales invoice as proof that you have paid VAT. As VAT is higher in Italy, you may be requested to pay the difference between the two rates when you cross the border. Televisions and music centres tend to cause problems at customs and duty may have to be paid. It should also be noted that British TV sets do not generally function satisfactorily in Italy. The same is true for UK portable telephones.

Do not bring lamps or lights with bayonet fittings, unless you are also prepared to bring a good supply of light bulbs with you, as only the screw-in type are sold in Italy. If you are bringing appliances with a built-in plug you will need an adaptor, as Italian plugs have two or three pins in a row.

Clothing and shoes
Italians live up to their reputation for chic fashion, and dress with great care and expense. The *passeggiata*, the evening stroll that most Italians take along a town's main *corso*, is an important social ritual. Appearance

is everything and designer labels score the highest marks. It is rare to see an Italian in a pair of patched jeans or an old jumper — unless of course it is part of a fashion statement. Casual dressing simply doesn't happen very much. By comparison most British visitors seem disastrously under-dressed and shabby.

If you have a limited budget you should bring as much clothing with you as possible, for other than outdoor markets there are few places to buy cut-price clothing. Sales, *saldi*, take place in January and early February, and also in late July and August before summer vacation begins. But even if there is a 50 per cent discount on a sweater that was £150 it still seems quite expensive by British high street standards. For a winter stay include a raincoat and a winter coat in your packing as winters can be surprisingly cold. If you have a fur coat this may be your best chance to wear it. Animal rights campaigners are not very active in Italy and few Italians have any compunction about wearing fur.

Sportswear is also something you should consider bringing with you as it, and sports equipment, is generally more expensive in Italy.

If you like to make your own clothes you may wish to bring paper patterns with you. The selection in Italy is restricted to Burda patterns and you may find the instructions stretch your Italian to its limit.

Babycare and children's clothing
The cost of clothing, toys, baby foods and babycare items is considerably higher in Italy than in the UK. You will find no equivalent to Mothercare, Boots, Early Learning or any other of the reasonably-priced chain stores that exist in Britain. Prenatal, one the biggest children's chains in Italy, has a full range of products, but prices are high. Therefore bring as much as possible with you, especially if there is food your child particularly enjoys. The selection of baby food is somewhat restricted and the Italian diet is very different to the British.

Food
Italians take immense pride and pleasure in their national cuisine, and ingredients for other cuisines are not widely available, so such things as spices and condiments should be brought with you. Cooking utensils such as woks and lidded saucepans with single handles are also not very commonplace.

Imported tea is available but is sold in small quantities at twice the UK price. Baking powder and icing sugar are also sold in very small quantities. Food colouring and many flavourings are not commonly available in Italy as they have been withdrawn for health reasons.

Books and stationery

A good supply of general reading material is a must, for unless you are in
a large city or a town with a high student population you will find English
books hard to come by. In the major cities there are of course bookshops
which carry reasonable selections of English literature and in Rome there
is a second-hand English book shop near the Opera.

Most stationery items are readily available, with the exception of
Blu-Tac. All computer services are also easily found, including those for
Amstrad, Phillips and Apple.

Pharmaceuticals and toiletries

If you take a regular prescribed drug bring a good supply in order to give
you time to locate its equivalent in Italy. Many drugs are marketed under
different names. Your doctor or the drug manufacturer should be able to
tell you the brand name used in Italy, and whether the formula given in
Italy is exactly the same as your current prescription.

The Bodyshop has branches in the major cities throughout Italy.
However, there is no real equivalent to Boots, and there are few toiletries
for the middle of the market. Most are sold in small boutiques which
specialise in designer brands, or in supermarkets alongside the bleach and
the toothbrushes. The same applies to cosmetics. Face flannels are not
used by Italians and are not easily available.

CHECKLIST OF ITEMS NOT READILY AVAILABLE IN ITALY

- wall-to-wall floor coverings
- window blinds
- secondhand furniture
- electric kettles
- woks
- lidded saucepans with a single handle
- oriental foods and spices
- reading material
- Blu-Tac
- face flannels.

HOW TO GET TO ITALY

By air

The fastest and in many cases the most economic way to travel to Italy is
by air, its only real disadvantage being that luggage allowances are

minimal. For this reason those setting up a holiday home will probably be wise to travel and transport their goods and chattels by car, perhaps in a number of stages. However, those setting up a permanent home might find the combination of an overland removals firm for the household goods and a cheap flight the best solution, as it avoids the problem of having to convert a UK-registered car into an Italian one. The normal baggage allowance on flights is 20kg per person, or 30kg if you are travelling first class, with excess baggage charged per kilo at first class travel rates.

The cost of air flights to Italy varies greatly, depending on the type of flight and ticket you book.

- A **normal return ticket** from the UK costs around £450, has no restrictions and is valid for one year.

- **Eurobudget** fares are less expensive, with a return to Rome costing around £390. With this type of ticket the return date may be left open.

- **Apex** tickets are one step lower, with a return fare to Rome in high season costing about £260 and in low season around £215. However, only return tickets are available and the dates of travel must be fixed. Another restriction is that at least one Saturday night must be spent in Italy.

- **Sunsavers,** the cheapest type of standard ticket, operate on a similar basis except that the reservation must be made at least 14 days before departure. A Sunsaver to Rome in high season costs about £226, and in low season it is about £183.

Direct flights from Britain are operated by Alitalia, British Airways, Aer Lingus, Air UK, Meridiana and Sabena:

Alitalia
205 Holland Park Avenue
London W11 4XB
Tel: (081) 745 8200.

British Airways
PO Box 10
Heathrow Airport London
Hounslow TW6 2JA
Tel: (081) 759 551.

Aer Lingus
Travel Shop 223 Regent Street
London W1
Tel: (081) 899 4747.

Air UK
Stansted House
Stansted Airport
Essex CM24 1QT
Tel: (0279) 680146.

Meridiana
15 Charles Street
London SW1 4QU
Tel: (071) 839 2222.

Sabena
36 Piccadilly
London W1
Tel: (081) 780 1444.

Most of these companies offer discounts of 25 per cent for travellers aged between 12 and 26. If you book a scheduled flight with Alitalia you will be eligible for the economy car hire, Jetdrive, which is offered by Avis, provided you rent the car for at least three days. For details of the numerous other companies offering cut-price charter flights it is best to consult your local travel agents or scan the classified columns in the newspapers as the operators change frequently.

The flight from London to Rome takes two-and-a-quarter hours. For destinations in the south of Italy one normally has to change at Rome or Milan, which means the flight can take up to three-and-a-half hours.

Italian airports
The principal Italian airports with regular scheduled and charter flights from Britain are as follows:

Alghero	Fertilia Airport
Bari	Palese Airport
Bologna	Borgo Panigale Airport
Brindisi	Papola Casale Airport
Cagliari	Elmas Airport

Catania	Fontanarossa Airport
Florence	Peretola Airport
Genoa	C. Colombo Sestri Airport
Milan	Linate and Malpensa Airports
Naples	Capodichino Airport
Palermo	Punta Raisi Airport
Pisa	Galileo Galilei Airport
Rome	Leonardo da Vinci and Fiumincino Airports
Turin	Caselle Airport
Venice	Marco Polo Tessera Airport

UK charter flights also make use of the following airports, although many are in operation during the summer season only:

Ancona	Falconara Airport
Bergamo	Orio al Serio Airport
Brindisi	Papola Casale Airport
Lamezia Terme	Santa Eufemia Airport
Olbia	Costa Smeralda Airport
Pescara	P. Liberi Airport
Rimini	Miramare Airport
Treviso	San Giuseppe Airport
Trieste	Ronchi del Legionari Airport
Verona	Valerio Catullo/Villafranca Airport

Flights from the USA
Those travelling from the USA may be able to use their Frequent Flyer Program. Otherwise a standard APEX return from New York to Rome costs approximately $900. Charter fares may be slightly lower; details can be found at your local travel agent or by scanning the adverts in the Sunday travel supplements. Airlines flying regularly from New York to Italy include Alitalia, Lufthansa and United Airlines:

Alitalia
666 Fifth Avenue
New York NY 10103
Tel: (212) 582 8900.

United Airlines
605 Third Avenue
New York NY 10016
Tel: (212) 290 2141.

Going by car

The journey from London to Rome is a somewhat gruelling 1800km, which normally involves about 20 hours of driving. It is best spread over two days as the quickest route, on the motorways, is really monotonous. Unless you are sharing the cost between four passengers, travelling by car is more expensive than flying, as on top of the basic fuel cost there is also the cross-channel ferry or train to pay for, motorway tolls in both France and Italy, as well as accommodation and other general travel expenses. The most direct and quickest route is by taking the short ferry crossing from Dover or Folkestone to Calais or Boulogne, then driving through France to Basel in Switzerland. At the Swiss border you will be requested to pay a tax which is levied on all Swiss road users and be presented with a sticker to display in your window, which permits you to use the Swiss road system for one year. Finally, from Switzerland head through the Alps via the Gotthard Tunnel to Milan. An alternative route is to take the longer ferry crossing to Ostend or Zeebrugge, and travel through Belgium and Germany where the motorways are free, although you will have to pay for the Brenner Autobahn in Austria.

Motorail

You may also wish to consider using the motorail service which operates in the summer from Boulogne to Milan. The journey takes about 15 hours and costs around £450 each way for car, driver, passenger and couchettes. For details apply to:

French Railways
179 Piccadilly
London W1V 0BA
Tel: (071) 409 3518.

By coach

The cost and time entailed in travelling to Italy by coach again make flying the more desirable option. A return ticket from London to Rome comes to around £135 and the journey from London to Turin, which is one of the closest destinations in Italy, takes approximately 28 hours. From London Victoria Coach Station the route passes via Dover, Paris, Mont Blanc and Aosta, from where the itinerary depends on your destination. Major destinations include Turin, Genoa, Milan, Venice, Bologna, Florence and Rome. For further details contact any National Express office in the UK or one of the addresses below:

National Express
Victoria Coach Station
Buckingham Palace Road
London SW1
Tel: (071) 730 0202.

Eurolines
52 Grosvenor Gardens
Victoria
London SW1
Tel: (071) 730 8235.

Going by train

Travelling by rail from Britain to Italy has the advantage of giving you
the opportunity to stop by at other destinations in Europe. Tickets issued
in Britain are valid for up to two months and have no restrictions on the
number of times you break your journey. If you intend to meander your
way to Italy you will find the *Thomas Cook Continental Timetable*
invaluable. It is published monthly, so make sure you get an up to date
version, and is available from any Thomas Cook branch or by post from:

Thomas Cook Timetable Publishing
PO Box 36
Peterborough

If you purchase an inter-rail card, available for young people up to 26
years old, you will travel free on railways in Italy until its expiry date. The
under 26s can also obtain discounts with a BIGE card, details from:

Eurotrain
52 Grosvenor Gardens
London SW1

or with a Transalpino card, details from:

71-75 Buckingham Palace Road
London SW1.

Senior Citizen cards are also valid in Italy and give you considerable
reductions.

A normal return ticket from London to Rome costs in the region of £200. You can expect to pay a supplement on top of this for a sleeping berth. A direct trip from London to Rome takes about 26 hours, the four commonest routes from London being as follows:

- London, Calais, Paris, Modena, Turin
- London, Calais, Switzerland, Chiassio, Milan
- London, Calais, Paris, French Riviera, Ventimiglia
- London, Ostend, Karlsruhe, Munich, Brenner.

The Orient Express
If you want to arrive in Italy in style there is always the Orient Express which runs from London to Venice via Paris and Milan. You can expect to pay from £700 upwards for a single journey, inclusive of meals. For further details contact the addresses below.

Sea Containers House
20 Upper Ground
London SE1 9PF
Tel: (071) 928 6000.

Orient Express Suite 1235
One World Trade Center
New York NY10048
Tel: (212) 938 6830.

Italian State Railway
Tickets can be booked for the Italian State Railway at the following address:

Marco Polo House
3/5 Lansdowne Road
Croydon
Surrey
Tel: (081) 686 0677.

Removals

If you are moving your household belongings from Britain to Italy you will probably be using an international removal firm. You are well advised to use one that takes responsibility for all the paperwork involved, which includes writing a full inventory in both English and Italian. Most removal firms also take charge of the packing and unpacking. The cost of the removal depends on the volume of your belongings. A full container load might cost around £2,500. However, if two or three households share a container you can save up to £600. The problem with sharing a container is waiting for other households in the same area. The most frequent removals are made to Northern Italy during the summer. Below are the head office addresses of some of the major international removal companies in Britain. Other companies can be found by simply looking in the *Yellow Pages*.

Allied Pickfords
Riverside House
Stonehill Business Park
Angel Road
London N18 3LD
Tel: (081) 807 2223.

Britannia
Serin House
Hindsley Place
London SE23 2NF
Freephone: (0800) 212024.

Scotpac
Kingsbridge Road
Barking
Essex
Tel: (081) 591 3388.

Trans Euro
Drury Way
Brent Park
London NW10 0JN
Tel: (081) 784 0100.

Interpack Worldwide Ltd
Unit 11 Hanover West Trading Estate
161 Acton Lane
London NW10
Tel: (081) 965 5550.

AGS International
2 Bush Industrial Estate
Standard Road
London NW10 6DF
Tel: (081) 961 7595.

CASE HISTORY: ARRIVING BY CAMPERVAN

Malcolm and Sandra came to Italy with a camper van, with the intention of buying a property, but before leaving the UK they failed to execute the necessary formalities, the V5, the V561 and the scheda tecnica. After purchasing their property they discovered exactly what was required and had to return to the UK to obtain the necessary documents. So far so good, even if the trip home was an unnecessary expense. They decided to apply for the scheda tecnica in Italy and managed to obtain it from the manufacturer, only to discover that their camper was classified as a van. The authorities in Italy didn't recognise the vehicle as being the same as that in the documents in which it is described as a camper. The result is that they were forced either to reimport it back to the UK (which was difficult as the exportation was never properly completed) or to drive it illegally in Italy and risk its confiscation and a hefty fine.

Moral: buy in Italy and don't attempt to import; or get your paperwork right at the very start.

3
How to Get Around

THE BEST FORMS OF TRANSPORT

The public transport system in Italy is well used and reasonably priced by European standards, but it is chaotic at the best of times. Probably the most efficient services are run by private transport companies which operate on a small local scale in towns and around their outlying villages. The railway system, which is for the most part state owned, suffers in the same way that most public services do in Italy. It seems to exist entirely for its own benefit, is inefficient and out of date. The ticket system is complicated, the trains are notoriously unpunctual and for a few days every so often the system is paralysed by strikes. Travelling by ferry, either between the mainland and Italian islands, or on internal waters, is both pleasant and fairly well organised. Those short of time can also take advantage of the extensive domestic airways network which operates regular flights between the major Italian cities.

Travelling by railway

The boot of Italy is almost completely girdled by railway tracks. This does little to enhance the coastline, but it makes for scenic train rides and preserves Italy's mountainous interior. The great majority of the network, which covers some 16,000km, is owned by the state and is known as the *Ferrovie Statale*. There are however a few private lines, such as that which rings Mount Vesuvius in Southern Italy.

The fares for travelling by train are calculated according to distance travelled, the type of train, and whether you choose a first or second class seat. Below is a list of the various types of trains, arranged in order of cost and speed at which they travel.

- ETR 450 Pendolino
- Intercity
- Express

● Diretto
● Locale

The ETR 450 Pendolino is a first class, high speed train for which reservations are obligatory. Seat reservation is also obligatory on Intercity trains, for which a supplementary charge of around 30 per cent of the cost of the fare is levied on most lines. The Express and Diretto also cover long distances but stop frequently, particularly the Diretto. The Locale only runs short distances and dawdles interminably at each station, as it usually has to give way to any train of a higher category and is frequently overtaken.

Seat reservations can be made from two months up to three hours before the time of departure, bookings being taken at the railway station or from an authorised travel agency. When you board the train you will find your seat is reserved with a card bearing your name. However, once the train has started reserved seats that are not occupied may be taken by other passengers. If you buy your ticket on the train you will have to pay a surcharge of 20 per cent.

Rail cards and economy tickets
Before booking a ticket you may wish to look into the various types of rail cards and economy tickets that exist.

● A **Carta Verde** is a youth rail card for people aged between 12 and 26 years. It offers a discount of 30 per cent for all the year except during Easter, Christmas and in the summer from 25th June to 31st August, when the discount is reduced to 20 per cent. Cards are issued with a validity of either one or three years. Those travelling to Greece by railway may also use the *Carta Verde* to obtain a 50 per cent discount on specified ferry crossings.

● If you are not a resident of Italy you can purchase an unlimited circulation tourist ticket, known as a **BTLC (Biglietto Turistico Libera Circolazione)**. This ticket gives unlimited travel on the State railway network for a period of 8, 15, 21 or 30 days, depending on the length of time you wish. You can travel in first or second class, there are no surcharges and seat reservations are not necessary.

● If you intend to cover great distances by rail you may be interested in the **chilometrico** ticket. The 'kilometric' ticket allows free travel for up to 3,000km and is valid for two months. It can be used by up to five people, but no more than 20 journeys can be made.

● Regular reduced fares are also offered to senior citizens and children under 12, while children under 4 who do not occupy a seat travel free.

● Discounts are also offered to families and parties of 10-20 people.

If you purchase a ticket but do not use it, it is possible to obtain a refund providing you return it to the station from which you bought it on the day for which your ticket is valid. For trains that are delayed for more than 29 minutes, refunds of any supplements or surcharges that have been paid are also offered. The refund will be given in the form of a coupon that can be used on subsequent rail travel.

Telephone numbers of the principal railway information offices are:

Bologna	(051) 372126	Padua	(049) 6161806
Bolzano	(0471) 24292	Palermo	(091) 230806
Cagliari	(070) 656293	Pisa	(050) 41385
Catania	(095) 531625	Prato	(0574) 26617
Florence	(055) 278785	Reggio Calabria	(0965) 98123
Genoa	(010) 284081	Rimini	(0541) 53512
Livorno	(0586) 401105	Rome	(06) 4775
Messina	(090) 775234	Savona	(019) 806969
Milan	(02) 67500	Turin	(011) 517551
Naples	(081) 5534188		

Travelling by coach and bus

Local bus networks operate in rural districts, connecting villages and towns. Tickets are available either from the bus station or on the bus itself. Buses also operate in inner city areas, where bus tickets are sold at major bus stations, *tabacchi* (tobacconists) and sometimes at newspaper kiosks: look for signs saying *'biglietti'*. Tickets are the same price wherever you travel within a city, but if you plan to use city buses regularly you may wish to buy a monthly season ticket *(abbonamento)*. Many cities also have trams which operate on the same ticket system as the buses. Rome, Milan and Naples have a *Metropolitana* (underground train) too. Tickets for the *Metropolitana* are sold at train stations and, like buses, have a flat-rate fare.

Express coach services connect the major cities as well as some of the smaller towns in Italy. Fares are relatively inexpensive and services are operated fairly frequently. Information on timetables is held at local tourist offices and sometimes at local police stations, as well as being posted up at the bus depot itself.

Some coach services also run guided tours both of the local vicinity and as long-distance journeys. The most popular coach trails take in Venice, Padua, Florence, Siena, Perugia, Assisi, Spoleto, Rome, Naples, Pompeii, Sorrento, Positano and Amalfi. Typical one-day itineraries are:

- Rome-Naples-Pompeii-Sorrento
- Venice-Padua-Florence, and
- Florence-Siena-Perugia-Assisi-Spoleto-Rome.

For further information you should contact the tourist information centre or a travel agent in the city in which you are staying.

Travelling by ferry

Italy has a good ferry network which operates around its 7,500km of coastline, to and from the two large islands Sardinia and Sicily, and across the northern lakes.

Sardinia and Sicily
The main crossings for Sardinia are:

- Genoa to Porto Torres/Olbia/Cagliari/Arbatax;
- Civitavecchia to Olbia/Cagliari/Arbatax/Golfo Aranci;
- Naples to Cagliari;
- Livorno to Porto Torres/Golfo Aranci/Olbia.

For Sicily the main crossings are:

- Genoa to Palermo;
- Naples to Palermo/Catania/Syracuse;
- Livorno to Palermo;
- Villa San Giovanni to Messina;
- Reggio Calabria to Messina.

There is also a hydrofoil service from Naples to Palermo three times a week, which takes 5 hours 20 minutes. It is also possible to travel from Cagliari in Sardinia to Palermo or Trapani in Sicily.

Below are the UK addresses of two of the principal ferry companies that connect mainland Italy to Sicily and Sardinia:

Tirrenia Line and Navarma
c/o Serena Holidays
40-42 Kenway Road
London SW5 0RA
Tel: (071) 373 6548.

Grandi Traghetti
Associated Oceanic Agencies
103-105 Jermyn Street
London SW1
Tel: (071) 930 5683.

From Sicily a ferry service operates from the northern coast to the Aeolian islands. The crossings are operated by the following companies:

Aliscafi Snav
Molo Norimberga 23
Messina
Tel: (090) 774862.

Siremar
Via Depretis 78
Naples
Tel: (081) 5512113.

The Bay of Naples
The Bay of Naples is criss-crossed by ferries operating between destinations either side of the bay, and between the mainland and small offshore islands. The principal crossings are:

● Naples to Capri/Ischia/Procida/Sorrento;
● Sorrento to Capri.

The companies making these crossings both by ferry and hydrofoil are:

Navigazione Libera del Golfo
Molo Beverello
Naples
Tel: (081) 5527209.

Caremar
Molo Beverello
Naples
Tel: (081) 5515384.

Linea Lauro
Molo Beverello
Naples
Tel: (081) 5513236.

Alilauro
Via Caracciolo 13
Naples
Tel: (081) 7611004.

Aliscafi Snav
Via Caracciolo 10
Naples
Tel: (081) 612348.

Elba
The island of Elba is serviced by car ferry from Piombino and Livorno,
and by hydrofoil from Piombino. The companies operating these services
are:

Navarma
Viale Elba 4
Portoferraio
Tel: (0565) 918101.

Toremar
Via Calafati 6
Livorno
Tel: (0586) 896113.

Toremar
Piazzale Premuda
Piombino
Tel: (0565) 31100.

Giglio
The island of Giglio which lies off the Etruscan coast, is connected by
car-ferry to Porto Santo Stefano by:

Toremar
Piazzale Candi
Porto Santo Stefano
Tel: (0564) 814615.

Maregiglio
Giglio Porto
Tel: (0564) 809309.

Adriatic coast
On the Adriatic coast the Adriatica Line runs ferries from Manfredonia, Vieste, Peschici, Rodi Garganico, and Termoli to the Tremiti islands. There is also a hydrofoil to the Tremiti islands from Ortona, Vasto and Termoli. The Adriatica Line is represented in the UK by Sealink:

Charter House
Park Street
Ashford
Kent
Tel: (0233) 647022.

Northern Lakes
The northern lakes are traversed by umpteen services, including hydrofoils, car-ferries and even steamers.

Lake Maggiore has regular ferries connecting Brissago, Cannobio, Luino, Verbania, Baveno, Stresa, Belgirate, Arona, Locarno, Laveno and others. There is also a hydrofoil service between Arona, Stresa and Locarno, and a car-ferry between Verbania, Intra and Laveno. Most services, as well as cruises on the lake, are operated by:

Navigazione Lago Maggiore
Via Baracca 1
Arona
Tel: (0322) 46651.

Lake Como has steamers, hydrofoils and car-ferries that connect Como, Cernobbio, Carate, Argegno, Tremesso, Cadenabbia, Bellagio, Menaggio, Varenna, Bellano, Colico and others. Most of these services are operated by:

Navigazione Lago Como
Via Rubini 22
Como
Tel: (031) 273324.

Lake Garda has frequent ferries and hydrofoils operating between Riva, Torbole, Limone, Malcesine, Brenzone, Gargnano, Maderno, Gardone, Salo, Garda, Bordolino, Sirmione, Desenzano and Peschiera. There is also a car-ferry between Maderno and Torri del Benaco. The main company running these services as well as cruises on the lake is:

Navigazione Lago Garda
Piazza Matteotti
Desenzano
Tel: (030) 9141321.

Lake Iseo is serviced by:

Cooperativa Operatori Turistici
Via Duomo 17
Iseo
Tel: (030) 981154.

Travelling by Air

The largest Italian air company, Alitalia, and its sister company Ati, operate domestic services between 26 cities in Italy, with the majority of flights centering on Rome and Milan. There are regular flights from Alghero, Bologna, Cagliari, Genoa, Naples, Olbia, Palermo, Pisa and Venice. Bookings are taken by authorised travel agents in almost any town or city. Before booking your flight check whether you are eligible for one of the following reductions:

- Families travelling together: 50 per cent.
- *'Nastro Verde'* flights at off-peak times: 30 per cent.
- Children up to 2 years old: 90 per cent.
- Children from 2 to 12 years old: 50 per cent.
- Young people aged 12-26: 25 per cent.
- Weekend return flights, travelling on a Saturday or a Sunday and with no more than four weeks interim: 30 per cent.
- Flights on Sundays, returning the same day: 50 per cent.
- Return flights from North to South Italy: 30 per cent.

The head offices for Alitalia and Ati are:

Alitalia
Palazzo Alitalia
Piazzale G. Pastore
EUR
Rome
Information, Tel: (06) 5456
Domestic flight reservations, Tel: (06) 5455.

Ati
Palazzo Ati
Aeroporto Capodichino
Naples
Information and reservations, Tel: (081) 7091111.

Travelling by taxi

Taxis are available in every Italian town. They are usually assembled in ranks in main piazzas, at railway stations and airports, but can also be called by phone. It is not, however, normal to hail a taxi as it passes by. Taxis charge different fares in different places. The fare, however, is always based on a fixed starting charge plus a rate per kilometre. The fixed starting charge at present ranges from Lit.2,800 to Lit. 6,400, while the rate per kilometre is generally between Lit.1,000 and Lit.1,250. Extra charges are made for services at night, and services on Sundays or public holidays. Surcharges are also made for trips outside of a town, such as to an airport, and for luggage.

Hitchhiking

Hitchhiking is fairly commonplace in Italy, especially with students, and it is relatively easy to get lifts. However, for a more reliable solution it is possible to contact one of a number of organisations that arrange for people to share rides and costs. Contact the following addresses for information on shared travel:

Torpedo Blu
Via Quattro Fontane 2
Rome
Tel: (06) 4746525.

Via Vai
Via dei Falisci 10
Rome
Tel: (06) 493241.

Associazione Universitaria
Via degli Zingari 11
Rome
Tel: (06) 47465250.

Associazione Viaggi e Passaggi
Via Col di Lana 14
Milan
Tel: (02) 8320543.

Aldebaran Interstop
Via di Citta 101
Siena
Tel: (0577) 280495.

Stop Phone
Piazza Chironi 8
Turin
Tel: (011) 747636.

Gulliver
Via Scortici 4
Perugia
Tel: (075) 66791.

Associazione Studenti
Via Zabarella 19
Padua
Tel: (049) 31262.

Ateneapoli
Via Tribunali 362
Naples
Tel: (081) 447824.

Allonsanfan
Via Guelfa 64
Florence
Tel: (055) 283395.

Agilulfo
Strada Incuria 26
Bari
Tel: (080) 545138.

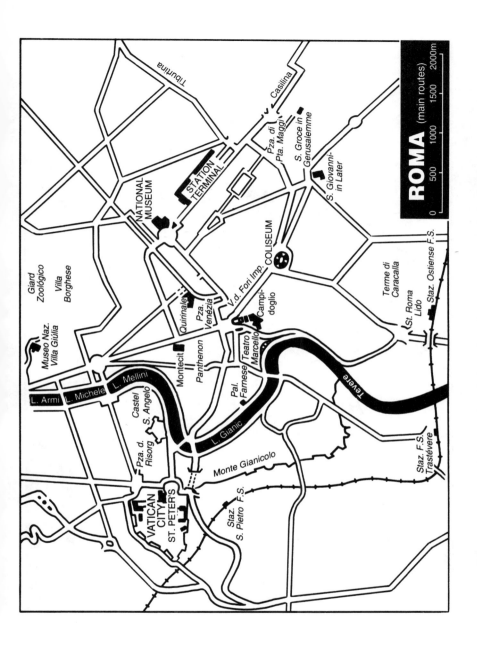

Fig. 2. Rome city plan.

43

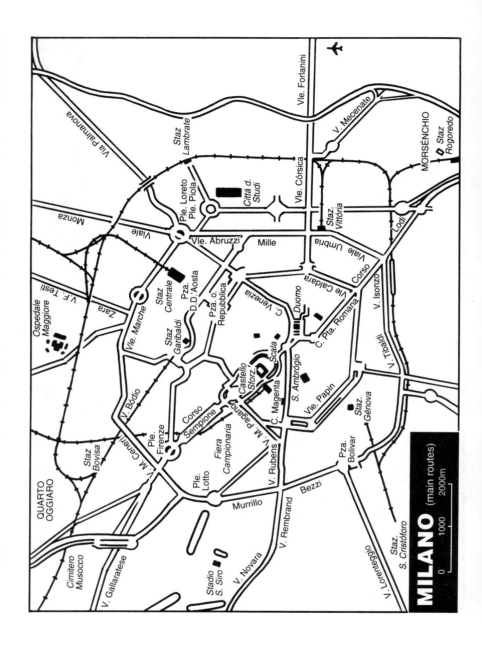

Fig. 3. Milan city plan.

44

DRIVING IN ITALY

'When in Rome do as the Romans do' is a saying that may conjure up nightmares when taken in the context of driving in Italy. Driving around in Italy requires a certain amount of bravery, a sharp wit and a good deal of patience. Speed, and small margins for error, seem to be the essence of Italian driving. Overtaking is perhaps the worst aspect, as it is done in dangerous situations with the overtaking driver one minute up your tail, and then a few centimetres to the left of your car, before he swerves in front of you nearly taking off your front bumper. Another nightmare of the road is the signposting. Signs are terrible and it can be enormously difficult to find the correct road, even with a good map. Quite often the junction is signposted only at the actual turning and not in advance, and there may be a display of 20 signs to scan through, including those for hotels, restaurants, businesses and public services. It is far from uncommon to find two signs for the same destination pointing in opposite directions; sometimes all roads do lead to Rome!

To add to this, most roads around big towns and cities are very busy, while the centres themselves are positively traffic-choked. Nearly all Italians have at least one car per family and many have two, or even three. Road congestion is not the only problem. Car parking is a headache almost everywhere, and when the winter brings fog and mist to the cities of Northern Italy there is the problem of car exhaust-enhanced smog too. When pollution levels reach an unbearable limit cars are restricted by allowing number plates ending in an even number on the roads one day and those ending in an odd number on the next. Sometimes vehicles are banned from using the roads altogether.

Getting around by car does, however, have its advantages, and if you intend to buy a rural property in Italy you may find that it is essential.

Hiring a car

Major international as well as Italian car-hire companies are represented at all airports and major railway stations throughout Italy, but in order to hire a car you must have had a full driving licence for at least one year. Most companies stipulate that the driver must be over 21 years old, and a new 1993 law states that drivers who have had their licences for less than three years are not allowed to drive vehicles with a speed capacity of over 150km per hour.

Hire rates vary from company to company and from car to car, but it is rarely cheap and you will be lucky if you can find a car for much under £200 per week. When you ask for a quote check that it includes breakdown service, maintenance, oil and basic insurance. Find out the cost of additional insurance, and remember that 19 per cent IVA (VAT) will be added to your final bill. It is normal for a company to ask for a deposit which is equal to the estimated cost of the car-hire. Car-hire firms in tourist centres and cities also usually rent out mopeds, motorbikes and sometimes bicycles too.

Maggiore, one of the largest Italian car-hire firms is represented in the UK at:

Transhire
Unit 16
88 Clapham Park Road
London SW4 7BX
Tel: (071) 978 1922.

Head offices of major car hire firms in Italy are:

Avis
Via Tiburtina 1231
Rome
Tel: (06) 4090960.

Hertz
Viale Leonardo da Vinci 421
Rome
Tel: (06) 51711.

Europcar
Via Lombardia 7
Rome
Tel: (06) 4750381.

Maggiore
Via Po 8a
Rome
Tel: (06) 858698.

Buying a car in Italy

In order to buy a car in Italy you must be registered as a local resident and be in possession of a **codice fiscale** (fiscal code number). You are well recommended to buy your car in the same region as that in which you are resident, for if you buy a car with a number plate which does not correspond to the province in which you are resident, you will have to change the number plates. This is a fairly lengthy and costly procedure (somewhere in the region of 900,000Lit. at present) and is best avoided. If you do end up buying a car which is not locally registered, the cost of changing the plates may be something you wish to negotiate with the dealer.

To exchange a car number plate go to the nearest Automobile Club Italiano (ACI), taking with you your *certificato residenza* (resident's certificate) and *codice fiscale* (fiscal code number). There may be an interim period in which your car has no number plate at all, as there is often a time gap between the surrender of the original plate and the arrival of the new one.

Another point to check before buying a car is whether its road tax has been paid. If a car has been off the road for some time, the chances are that the road tax payments have not been maintained. If this is the case you will find that you are liable for back payments when you go to renew the road tax.

The procedure for buying a car is quite straightforward. You will need to present your resident's certificate and fiscal code number. If you are buying a car privately take these documents and go to a local office of the Automobile Club Italiano (ACI) with the seller. The necessary documents will be drawn up for the transfer of ownership.

If you are a non-resident you can only purchase a brand new vehicle which is intended for export within a year of purchase. Failure to export in time can result in the vehicle being seized and the driver given a hefty fine.

Running a car in Italy

The two major costs involved in running a car in Italy, other than fuel, repair and maintenance, are insurance and road tax (car MOTs do not exist).

Insurance

Every vehicle must have basic third party insurance, proof of which is displayed in the car windscreen. Car insurance is obtainable from the Automobile Club Italiano and from insurance agents.

There are two types of insurance, *franchigia* and *bonus/malus*. The former type of policy is now less common and is only offered by the largest insurance companies and to heavy goods vehicles. A *franchigia* policy means that the driver pays for damage costs up to a certain amount, over and above which the insurance company takes responsibility. Far more common is the *bonus/malus* policy which operates on a no claims bonus system. A new driver starts with 18 points, others enter at number 14 and for each year that you do not claim you lose a point. If you have an accident you gain two points.

The obligatory basic insurance only offers third party and members of family who are travelling in the car. The driver is covered by taking out a supplement for *conducente anonimo* (unnamed driver) which will also pay for hospital treatment in case of an accident. Insurance against theft and fire put up the cost of the policy considerably. However, if you are in a city, particularly in the South of Italy, it is probably worth paying for as car theft is very commonplace. In the large Italian cities there is one car stolen every 90 seconds. The city of Cagliari in Sardinia is said to be the most active centre, as vehicles are shipped out from there to Turkey and the Gulf. You may also be interested to know that Fiat 500s and Fiat Unos are especially popular with car thieves.

Road tax
Road tax is payable every three, six or 12 months at your local **PTT** (post office). The *bollo* (chit) with which you make the payment is available from Automobile Club Italiano (ACI) offices. However, if your car has been in circulation in Italy for any length of time you should have received a supply of *bolli* (chits) in the form of a large cheque book. Each *bollo* is valid for three months. The *bollo* should be renewed within the first two weeks following the month of expiring, ie if it is valid for October, then the next tax must be paid by the 14th November. The *bollo* must be filled in using the information on the charts you will find up on the wall in any post office, the idea being to calculate the amount of tax you must pay. This depends on the type of fuel that is used, the horsepower category of the engine and the length of time for which you wish to tax the car. There is also an additional tax for car radios and cassette players. See the model *bollo* on page 50.

Once your *bollo* is completed take it to any counter that is not reserved for postal transactions and pay the final figure. You will be given a receipt which acts as your tax disc and must be displayed alongside your insurance in your windscreen.

If you are still in the process of converting your British-registered car to Italian plates and your British road tax has expired, you should apply to an Automobile Club Italiano (ACI) office for a temporary road tax cover. This costs considerably less than the full road tax. However, in theory it can only be issued for three months, although in practice it seems it can be renewed almost indefinitely.

Fuel

There are two grades of petrol available in Italy: *benzina normale*, which has an octane rating of 85-88, and *benzina super* which has an octane level of 98-100. Lead free petrol, *verde* or *senza piombo*, is also sold at most garages although it has a lower octane level than that sold in the UK and you may find your car will not perform as it should. *Verde verde*, a lead free petrol with a higher octane level of around 95 is a better option, but it is not very widely available. All types of petrol are expensive by British standards. *Benzina super* is about 1550Lit. per litre and *verde* is around 1500Lit. per litre. Diesel is not as expensive and costs around 1100Lit. per litre. Diesel cars (which are not classified as commercial vehicles), however, are not cheap to run if you are an Italian resident, as a high road tax is levied on them. It is only more economic to run a diesel car if you cover more than 20,000 kilometres a year.

Opening hours of petrol stations do vary from place to place, but in general most open from 7.30 am to 12.30 pm and then take two or three hours for lunch, re-opening around 3 pm until 7 pm. Only 25 per cent of petrol stations are open on Sundays and public holidays. Many are closed on Mondays too or for one other week day. However, petrol stations on motorways, which can be found every 25km, stay open 24 hours a day. Some non-motorway petrol stations also have automatic pumps which operate 24 hours a day and accept 10,000Lit. notes.

WHAT ARE THE RULES OF THE ROAD?

Road regulations

The first thing to remember about driving in Italy is to keep to the right-hand side of the road and give way to traffic from the right on roundabouts and at crossroads. If you have a right-hand drive car you will find the left-hand wing mirror indispensable; it is anyway obligatory to have one. It is also obligatory to carry a warning triangle in your boot and to have your driving licence and car registration documents on you at all times.

Road signs are international and driving rules conform to European standards, although in practice little regard is given to pedestrian crossings, and traffic from the right often takes precedence. The degree to which driving rules are obeyed and enforced varies greatly across the country. Naples can seem to be virtually law-free at times, with neither traffic lights nor one-way streets being respected.

Children under 4 must be strapped into a car safety seat, and children

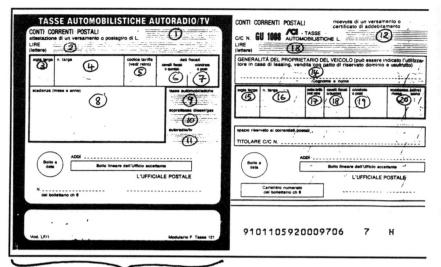

PART TO BE DISPLAYED IN CAR WINDSCREEN.

1. Total amount of tax paid in numerals.
2. Total amount of tax paid in letters.
3. Initials of province on number plate.
4. Number plate.
5. Tariff code.
6. Horse power.
7. Number of cylinders.
8. Expiry date.
9. Car tax.
10. Extra tax for diesel or gas
11. Tax for car radio or TV.
12. As 1.
13. As 2.
14. Surname and name of car owner.
15. As 3.
16. As 4.
17. As 5.
18. As 6.
19. As 7.
20. Expiry date (month & year).
21. Total amount of tax paid in numerals.

Form for paying car tax.

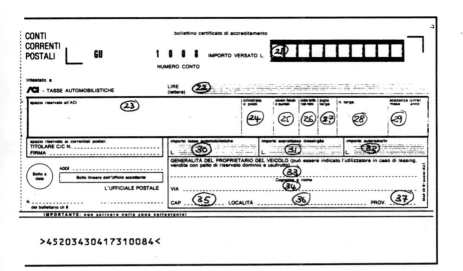

22. Total amount of tax paid in letters.
23. Space reserved for ACI (Automobile Club Italiano).
24. As 7.
25. As 6.
26. As 5.
27. As 3.
28. As 4.
29. As 20.
30. As 9.
31. As 10.
32. As 11.
33. As 14
34. Address - Street.
35. Post Code.
36. Place.
37. Province

aged between four and 12 must wear a child's safety restraint. Drunken driving is a grave offence, although breathalising is nothing like as common as in the UK and safe limits do not really exist. Fines are paid on the spot, usually after the driver has pleaded innocence and tried to knock down the cost of the fine. If you are unable to pay a fine you are given 60 days in which to honour your debt. A list of the most common offences and the fines they incur is given below.

Speeding up to 10km/h above the limit:	50,000Lit.
Speeding up to 40km/h above the limit:	200,000Lit.
Speeding 40km/h above the limit:	500,000Lit.
	plus suspension of licence
Driving on wrong side of road on a bend or in a place with poor visibility:	200,000Lit.
	plus suspension of licence
Not observing road signs:	50,000Lit.
Not giving way:	100,000Lit.
Going through a red light:	100,000Lit.
Overtaking on the inside:	50,000Lit.
Overtaking on a bend or hill:	100,000Lit.
Not maintaining a safe distance:	50,000Lit.
Misuse of lights:	100,000Lit.
Changing direction without signalling:	50,000Lit.
Disturbing the peace:	50,000Lit.
Stopping at a forbidden place:	50,000Lit.
Carrying more passengers than permitted:	50,000Lit.
Carrying a passenger on a moped:	50,000Lit.
Under-age driving	Seize vehicle
Not wearing a helmet:	50,000Lit.
Now wearing a safety belt:	50,000Lit.
Not carrying licence or circulation documents:	50,000Lit.
Carrying an out of date licence:	200,000Lit.
	plus withdrawal of licence

Speed limits

Speed limits are marked on road signs and should be observed carefully, although they rarely are by Italians. The limits are:

● in built-up areas 50km per hour;
● on country roads 90km per hour;

- on the motorway: for cars up to 1100cc and motorcycles up to 350cc 110km per hour; for cars over 1100cc and motorcycles over 350cc 130km per hour;
- towing a caravan or trailer: outside built-up areas 80km per hour; on the motorways 100km per hour.

Different limits are often set for weekends and public holidays. For variations in speed limits watch out for the illuminated signs on motorways, which also indicate road and traffic conditions, etc.

Drivers help one another not to be caught speeding by flashing their lights when the police are around on most roads, but on motorways of course this is not possible and automatic speed traps are used. The automatic detector photographs the speeding vehicle and dispatches a fine through the post. However, with the Italians' uncanny knack of wriggling out of most situations, the driver often denies responsibility, since the detector records the number plate and not the identity of the driver. The fine is payable by the person under whose name the vehicle is registered, not who was driving. A great number of high-power cars are therefore registered under the names of the geriatric members of a family. Hence Italy has a record high number of law-breaking elderly people.

Parking

Finding a place to park is a problem in all Italian towns and cities. The medieval streets that characterise so many of Italy's towns were not designed to accommodate the hordes of cars that now flood them. Parking meters are often posted along narrow streets that radiate out from the town centre, but these spaces are invariably full. Small fee-paying car-parks are also usually dotted around a centre, but like parking meters there is generally a 90-minute limit and the spaces are quickly filled. You will also find areas that are marked *zona disco or zona blu*. A **disco** is a parking disc with a clock face on which you can indicate the time you arrived. If you do not have one, apply to the Automobile Club Italiano (ACI), the tourist office or a petrol station. Parking in a *zona disco* obliges you to use the disc and to return within the time limit that is indicated, which varies from 20 minutes to an hour. The actual centre of many towns is closed to all traffic during working hours, except for residents and public transport. This exacerbates the parking problem, but of course makes for blissfully traffic-free town centres. In the centre of Rome parking is strictly prohibited on weekdays and is indicated by signs reading *zona tutelato*. In Florence all vehicles are banned from the centre from 7.30 am to 6.30 pm on weekdays except for access. Venice has overcome its parking problems

COMUNE DI FABRIANO

CORPO VIGILI URBANI

№ 08997 |7|

DI PROTOCOLLO

(1) In data | | | | | | | | i... **sottoscritt... vigil... urban.... ha...... accertato**

giorno | mese | anno | **a carico del veicolo contrassegnato** (7)

1 ☐ (2) **Autovettura** 2 ☐ (3) **Autobus** 3 ☐ (4) **Autocarro** 4 ☐ (5) **Rimorchio** 5 ☐ (6) **Moto ciclo** 6 ☐ **Moto carro**

(8) | | | | | | | | (9) | | | | | | | (10) | | | (11) | | | | |

FABBRICA — TIPO (12) — PROV. — TARGA

IN LOCALITÀ | | | | | | | | | | | | | | | | ALTEZZA N. CIVICO

alle ore | | | | (13) ore | minuti **l'infrazione sottoindicata:**

(14) ☐ 4012 Sostava in località vietata
(15) ☐ 4023 Sostava durante le ore di divieto
(16) ☐ 4034 Sost. dal lato vietato nella via con sosta giorni alterni
(17) ☐ 4045 Sostava nello spazio riservato ai taxi
(18) ☐ 4056 Sost. nello spazio di ferm. dei mezzi in serv. pubbl.
(19) ☐ 4060 Sost. oltre il tempo stabilito nel parcheg. regolamen.
(20) ☐ 4071 Sostava in zona disco orario con disco non esposto
(21) ☐ 4082 Sostava in zona disco orario oltre il tempo scadenza
(22) ☐ 4093 Sostava in zona disco orario con impiego disco errat.
(23) ☐ 4104 Transitava in zona vietata alla circolazione
(24) ☐ 4141 Sostava fuori dagli spazi delimitati
(25) ☐ 4126 Transitava in senso vietato
(26) ☐ 4130 Non si arrestava al segnale di stop all'incrocio
(27) ☐ 4734 Sostava in zona interdetta alla circolaz. dei veicoli
(28) ☐ 4200 Sostava inoperosamente in zona di carico e scarico
(29) ☐ 4211 All'incrocio ometteva di dare la dovuta precedenza
(30) ☐ 4362 Sostava senza esporre biglietto orario bollettatrice

(31) ☐ 115021 Sost. non lasciando spazio al transito di veicoli
(32) ☐ 115032 Sostava in prossimità di un incrocio
(33) ☐ 115043 Sostava in corrispondenza dell'incrocio
(34) ☐ 115054 Sostava distante dal margine della carreggiata
(35) ☐ 115076 Sostava sull'attraversamento pedonale
(36) ☐ 115080 Sostava allo sbocco di passo carrabile
(37) ☐ 115091 Sostava a fianco di altri veicoli
(38) ☐ 115102 Sostava con le ruote sul marciapiede
(39) ☐ 115430 Sostava nell'isola pedonale
(40) ☐ 115065 Sostava non parallelo all'asse stradale
(41) ☐ 115124 Sostava a sinistra rispetto alla direzione di marcia
(42) ☐ 4325 Sost. in zona vietat. per mercato il sabato mattina
(43) ☐ 4830 Sostava nello spazio riservato agli invalidi
(44) ☐ 112011 Transitava producendo forti rumori molesti
(45) ☐ 4406 Usufruiv. arbitr. rinn. period. sosta L.122 art.14 c.3
(46) ☐ 114015 Si fermava causando intralcio alla circolazione
(47) ☐ 134013 Non dava la prec. ai pedoni sull'attravers. pedon.

☐ | | | | | | | | | |
☐ | | | | | | | | | |
☐ | | | | | | | | | |

CONCILIABILE con L. | | | | | | (48) entro 60 gg. dall'accertamento presso il Comando della Polizia Municipale di Fabriano o con versamento su c/c postale n. 16690604 intestato al Comando Vigili Urbani di Fabriano, indicando nella causale il numero di protocollo del presente avviso.

I... **VERBALIZZANT...**

| | | | | | | |
| | | | | | | |

Fig. 5. Parking ticket and parking offences.

1. Date
2. Car
3. Bus
4. Lorry
5. Trailer
6. Motorbike
7. Three-wheeler van
8. Make of car
9. Model of car
10. Province
11. Number plate
12. Where parked
13. Time parked
14. Parked in forbidden place
15. Parked during forbidden times
16. Parked on forbidden side of road where parking is only permitted on alternate days
17. Parked in space reserved for taxis
18. Parked in space reserved for public transport
19. Parked outside times stipulated by car park
20. Parked in 'disc zone' without displaying disc
21. Parked in 'disc zone' after permitted time has expired
22. Parked in 'disc zone' with disc incorrectly adjusted
23. Crossed zone forbidden to traffic
24. Parked outside of lines marking a parking space
25. Entered a one-way street in the wrong direction
26. Not stopped at crossroads with a stop sign
27. Parked in an area forbidden to traffic
28. Parked in a place for loading or unloading
29. Not giving way at crossroads
30. Parked without displaying car-parking ticket
31. Parked without leaving room for traffic to pass
32. Parked near a crossroads
33. Parked in correspondence to a crossroads
34. Parked too far from the side of the road
35. Parked on a pedestrian crossing
36. Parked at the entrance to a right of way
37. Parked alongside another vehicle
38. Parked with wheels on pavement
39. Parked on a pedestrian island
40. Parked without being parallel to the road
41. Parked on the left against the direction of oncoming traffic
42. Parked in forbidden zone where there is a Saturday Market
43. Parked in a space reserved for invalids
44. Disturbing the public peace
45. Arbitrary penalty according to L./22 art. 14c3
46. Stopped, causing an interruption to the flow of traffic
47. Not giving way to pedestrians on a pedestrian crossing
48. Amount due

by building multi-storey carparks which are linked by ferry and bus services to destinations in Venice, but charges are exorbitant. Most large cities also have private garages which rent out space by the day and guarantee the safety of your car. Car parks with a custodian offer the same security, with fees usually charged by the hour. If you park your car at the side of a road make sure it is on the right side and facing the oncoming traffic.

Do not park where you see the signs *passo carrabile, divieto di sosta,* or *sosta vietato* as this means you will be blocking an entrance or a right of way. Neither should you park where you see the sign *zona rimozione* which means you car will be towed away. Should your car be towed away, go to the *Vigili Urbani* (police). You will be charged around Lit.100,000 to reclaim it, plus a fee for its storage.

If you receive a parking ticket take it to the police station, or pay a policeman on duty. The fine should be paid within 60 days. An example of a parking ticket is given in Figure 5 and shows a list of typical offences, each of which incurs a charge of up to Lit.100,000. You should also note the new parking regulation which states that where there is no pavement drivers must park 1m from the side of the road in order to allow pedestrians a right of way.

Car theft

If you have your car stolen while you are in Italy you should go to the nearest police station. The thieves may try to intervene before you get to the police and offer to return your car for a sum of money. However, accepting bribes does not secure the safe return of your vehicle. At the police station you will have to complete a *denuncia* which is a legal report that will eventually be read before a court of justice if necessary. You will not be able to make an insurance claim in Italy until the court has decreed the vehicle as stolen; until that point it is merely missing. Should your car be found again, the police will keep it impounded until you are ready to collect it. Before taking your vehicle back you will have to go to the police and complete another *denuncia*, stating that the vehicle has been re-covered. If the vehicle has any damage make sure that it is written on this report as this will enable you to make an insurance claim.

Motorways

Italy has a good network of motorways, covering over 6000km. Tolls are charged on all motorways except the one between Salerno and Reggio Calabria, which is also one of the most spectacular in Italy, those in Sicily between Palermo and Mazara del Vallo, and some short sections outside some of the larger cities.

Motorways are indicated by green signposts with white lettering, the particular motorway being designated by 'A' for *autostrada*, followed by the motorway number. Care should be taken on the motorways themselves, as often the exit signs appear only seconds before, or even at, the exit itself which can make for some rapid manoeuvering.

Before joining a motorway you must take a ticket from an automatic dispenser. Keep the ticket carefully as it has to be presented when you come off the motorway. The toll is calculated according to the type of vehicle you are travelling in and the distance you have covered. If you lose your ticket you will be charged for the maximum possible distance travelled on that motorway. If you intend to use the motorway regularly you may wish to purchase a **Viacard** which can be used for automatic payment. *Viacards* are available from the motorway toll booths and service areas, Automobile Club Italiano (ACI), and at *tabacchi* (tobacconists) in major towns. The cards are sold in denominations of 50,000Lit. and 90,000Lit. and the card is valid until the credit is used up. In order to pay with a *Viacard* get in the correct lane at the toll station and feed the card into the automatic machine. At toll stations without automatic barriers simply hand the card to the attendant.

If you break down on the motorway, make sure your hazard lights are on and your warning triangle is positioned at least 150m from your vehicle before heading for one of the SOS call boxes which are located at intervals of 2km. There are two types of call boxes; one is a regular phone into which you can speak, the other is a press button device which gives you the choice of alerting either the mechanical breakdown service or the Red Cross for ambulance service. The Automobile Club Italiano also operate a breakdown service which can be called by dialling 116.

Information on road conditions is transmitted by the radio stations RAI 1, 2 and 3 at half-hourly intervals in French, German and English. The reports are known as *Onda Verde* and *Onda Verde Europa* and are transmitted on frequencies FM and AM 103.5. Information is also broadcast through the televideo channel on TV, page 485 for normal road conditions, and page 495 for motorway conditions. By telephone dial (06) 43632121 or (06) 43634363 for the latest road reports. You will also find information in service areas where there is a televideo screen and the *Punti Blu* which are indicated by a large blue dot. When driving conditions are abnormal overhead signs are illuminated on the motorway itself and at the entry point to the system.

Most motorway service stations have snack-bars. The system is to go to the cash till before consuming anything, collect a receipt for the things you want to buy, then present the receipt to the bar-person who will make up your order. Service stations have restaurants, toilets, telephones and sometimes shops selling local produce.

Italian motorways
A comprehensive list of Italy's motorways is given below:

A1	Milan-Rome-Naples (Autostrada del Sole)
A3	Naples-Salerno-Reggio Calabria (Autostrada del Sole)
A4	Turin-Trieste (Serenissima)
A5	Turin-Aosta
A6	Turin-Savona
A7	Milan-Genoa
A8	Milan-Varese (Autostrada dei Laghi)
A9	Milan-Como-Chiasso (Autostrada dei Laghi)
A10	Genoa-Ventimiglia (Autostrada dei Fiori)
A11	Florence-Pisa (Firenze Mare)
A12	Genoa-Rome (Autostrada Azzurra)
A13	Bologna-Padua
A14	Bologna-Bari-Taranto (Autostrada Adriatica)
A15	Parma-La Spezia (Autostrada della Cisa)
A16	Naples-Bari (Autostrada dei due Mari)
A18	Messina-Catania
A19	Palermo-Catania
A20	Messina-Buonfornello
A21	Turin-Piacenza-Brescia (Autostrada dei Vini)
A22	Brennero-Modena (Autostrada del Brennero)
A23	Udine-Tarvisio (Autostrada Alpe-Adria)
A24	Rome-l'Aquila-Teramo
A25	Rome Pescara
A26	Genoa-Gravellona (Autostrada dei Trafori)
A27	Venice-Vittorio Veneto (Autostrada d'Alemagna)
A28	Portogruaro-Pordenone
A29	Palermo-Mazara del Vallo
A30	Caserta-Nola-Salerno
A31	Vicenza-Rovigo (Autostrada della Valdastico)
A32	Turin-Bardonecchia
T1	Traforo del Monte Bianco
T2	Traforo del Gran San Bernardo
T4	Traforo del Frejus

Italian road signs

Some of the most common road signs are:

entrata	entrance
incrocio	crossroads
lavori in corso	road works ahead
passaggio a livello	level crossing
pericolo	danger
rallentare	slow down
senso vietato	no entry
senso unico	one way
sosta autorizzata	Parking permitted at indicated times
sosta vietato	no parking
strada privata	private road
uscita	exit
vietato ingresso	no entry
vietato transito autocarri	closed to heavy vehicles.

CASE HISTORY: CATCHING THE FERRY

A family booked tickets for the ferry to Elba, but made a mistake with their dates, so that the rented accommodation dates did not correspond to those of the ferry dates. Unsure of what to do they contemplated trying to explain what had happened to the ferry company, but remembering that they were in Italy they decided to play it another way. They roughed up their ticket a bit so that the date was indistinct and turned up very early on the day they wished to travel back to mainland Italy, rather than on the day they had booked. There was the usual confusion at the ferry terminal and not only did they get to travel when they wanted, but even boarded an earlier ferry than they should have.

Moral: honesty is not *always* the best policy!

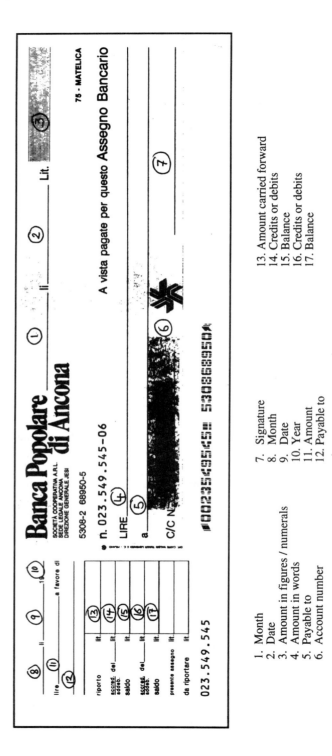

Fig. 6. Filling in an Italian cheque.

1. Month
2. Date
3. Amount in figures / numerals
4. Amount in words
5. Payable to
6. Account number

7. Signature
8. Month
9. Date
10. Year
11. Amount
12. Payable to

13. Amount carried forward
14. Credits or debits
15. Balance
16. Credits or debits
17. Balance

4
Practical Matters

DAY-TO-DAY LIVING

Banks and money

Although the banking system in Italy is somewhat antiquated, the pressure of the European Community free market has obliged banks to develop computer link-ups and install automatic cash machines to deal with everyday transactions. The banking system is still limited, however, by virtue of the fact that the majority of banks are local and not national. There are therefore difficulties in obtaining services at any other bank than your own, the branches of which are probably limited to the province or region. A credit card, Eurocheques, or travellers' cheques are therefore essential when travelling.

To open a bank account you will have to meet the bank manager, or his secretary, and if you can arrange for someone to introduce you or recommend you, all the better. You have to win the confidence of the bank manager, which means letting him get to know you, because the bank can find itself responsible for your personal debts. As well as being asked questions about yourself, you will probably have to show your resident's certificate, your fiscal code card and your passport.

Once you have a current bank account you may wish to request an automatic cash card, such as Bancomat, and a cheque book. Cheques have a limited value as they are often not accepted by people who do not know you, especially outside your own region. More versatile is a credit/charge card, such as Carta Si, which is very flexible but comes with an annual charge.

If you have an Italian cheque book fill it in as shown in figure 6. You will find that it is very common to leave who the cheque is payable to and also the date blank. You should also write *non-trasferibile* across the back of the cheque.

A bank account can be used to pay standing charges, such as telephone, electricity and gas bills, and to receive bank transfers from an overseas

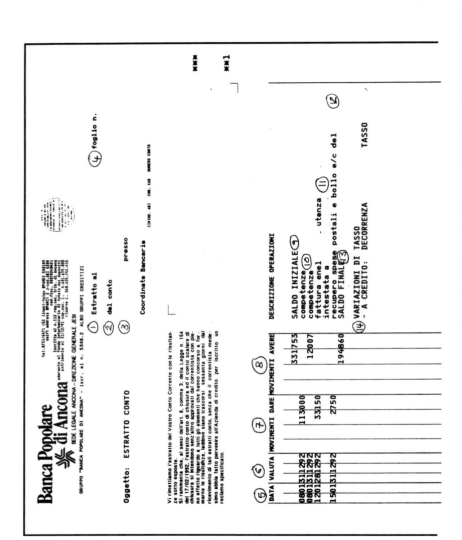

Banca Popolare di Ancona

tel. 0731/4471 152 linee - telex BPANS 560189
swift address BNCO IT 21 xxx cod./fisc. 00072920421
iscritta al tribunale di Ancona
patrimonio al 31/12/91 cap.soc. L. 264.639.300
riserve L. 264.639.300

SEDE LEGALE ANCONA – DIREZIONE GENERALE JESI

GRUPPO "BANCA POPOLARE DI ANCONA" – iscr. al n. 5308.2 ALBO GRUPPI CREDITIZI

① Estratto al

② del conto

④ foglio n.

Oggetto: ESTRATTO CONTO

③ presso

Coordinate Bancarie   CIN COD. ABI   COD. CAB   NUMERO CONTO

xxx

xx1

Vi rimettiamo l'estratto del Vostro Conto Corrente con le risultanze sotto esposte.
Si rammenta che, ai sensi dell'art. 8, comma 3, della Legge n. 154 del 17/02/1992, l'estratto conto di chiusura ed il conto scalare di chiusura si intendono senz'altro approvati dal correntista con pieno effetto riguardo a tutti gli elementi che hanno concorso a formarne le risultanze, laddove siano trascorsi sessanta giorni dal ricevimento di tali estratti conto, senza che il correntista medesimo abbia fatto pervenire all'Azienda di credito per iscritto un reclamo specificato.

⑤ DATA	⑥ VALUTA	⑦ MOVIMENTI DARE	MOVIMENTI AVERE ⑧	DESCRIZIONE OPERAZIONI
08013112 92			331753	SALDO INIZIALE ⑨
08013112 92		113000		competenze ⑩
12012812 92		33150	12007	competenze ⑩
				fattura enel – utenza ⑪
				intestata a
15013112 92		2750	194860	recupero spese postali e bollo e/c del
				SALDO FINALE ⑬
				⑭ VARIAZIONI DI TASSO
				– A CREDITO: DECORRENZA TASSO ⑮

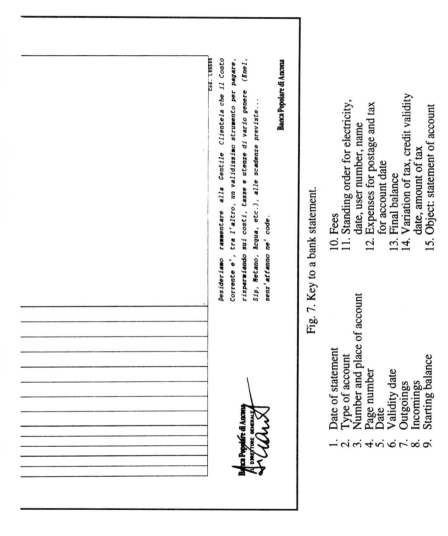

Fig. 7. Key to a bank statement.

1. Date of statement
2. Type of account
3. Number and place of account
4. Page number
5. Date
6. Validity date
7. Outgoings
8. Incomings
9. Starting balance
10. Fees
11. Standing order for electricity, date, user number, name
12. Expenses for postage and tax for account date
13. Final balance
14. Variation of tax, credit validity date, amount of tax
15. Object: statement of account

account. The disadvantages of opening a bank account are the numerous charges and taxes that are automatically deducted every year. A regular annual tax of around 20 per cent is directly debited, while an annual interest of around 3.5 per cent is credited. Commission is usually charged at about 0.5 per cent. It is also normal to pay for each cheque you write, as well as the cheque book itself and credit card transactions. Added to this there are *straordinario* (extraordinary) charges, such as when, in the summer of 1992, recession hit Italy and the Government levied a tax of 0.6 per cent on all current accounts. You may decide in the end to do without an Italian bank account altogether! All charges and other transactions are written on a monthly statement. The facsimile in Figure 7 may help you to decipher it.

If you are not a resident of Italy it is possible to open a foreigners' account. However, charges and taxes are higher than those for residents and should most definitely be checked beforehand. You should also check the facilities that are available. It is not, for example, possible to pay standing charges with a foreigners' account.

Most banks are open Monday to Friday 8.30 am - 1.30 pm and 3-4 pm, but hours do vary slightly from bank to bank, and some do not re-open in the afternoon at all. Every bank has an individual security door mechanism which involves pressing buttons, waiting before being able to enter, and passing through a metal detector (there are usually boxes in which to deposit metal objects such as car keys, etc). Inside the bank, money is handled at a reinforced-glass *cassa*, cash desk, while transactions are dealt with over the counter. This means that once you have completed a transaction you must then queue at the cash desk if you are receiving money.

Post offices

The PTT or *Ufficio Postale*, as the post office is called in Italy, is the nerve centre of Italian bureaucracy. It is here that you queue for your pension, your car tax, telephone and electricity bills and any of the miscellany of taxes that are payable by postal order. The post office of course also operates a variety of postal services which are usually available at a separate desk. If you simply want to buy a postage stamp *(francobollo)* you will probably find it quicker to go to a *tabacchi* (tobacconists), although if the letter is to be sent at a special rate the tobacconists may not be able to deal with it. Tobacconists do not deal with parcels either. To send a parcel you must fill in a form at the post office giving details of both the sender *(mittente)* and the receiver *(destinatario)*. If the parcel is to be sent overland, you may have to go to the parcel section of the post office. Most post offices are fussy about the way in which you package a parcel: the preferred method is to use string and a metal seal which can be purchased from a *cartolibreria* (book shop) or *tabacchi* (tobacconists).

Other services offered by the post office include sending telegrams and receiving mail by *poste restante* To receive correspondence by *poste restante* the sender should write *fermo posta* before the address of the post office. The post office also deals with money orders of various types. Authorised international reimbursements (ARI) and guaranteed payment papers (CPG) can be arranged telegraphically or by normal post, as well as international money orders. In order to cash money orders you will need to show your passport or identity card.

Information regarding postal services is obtainable by dialing 160.

Public telephones

Telephone booths are found in all town centres and in or near major post offices. Public telephones are also installed in cafes, and in remote country areas you will find authorised persons who have a phone for public use — look for the telephone symbol fixed to their house.

In order to operate a pay-phone you need either coins of Lit.100, 200 or 500 denominations, or a **gettone** (telephone token) which has a value of Lit.200, or a phone card. Phone cards, which are sold for Lit.5,000 or Lit.10,000, and *gettone* are available from *tabacchi* (tobacconists) or from SIP *(Societa Italiana Telefoni Pubblici)* offices. *Gettone* are also often used as currency and you may find them given to you in change. Phones in cafes and private homes usually operate on meters. The cost of the call is calculated by the number of *scatti* (points) that are registered on the meter. Cafes also sometimes add a supplementary charge for the use of the phone. The dialling tone sounds 'tu-tuuu'. When you hear 'tuuu' repeated at intervals it means the number is ringing. The continuous sound 'tu-tu-tu' means the number is engaged.

The charges made for using the telephone depend on the time of day and the distance. The categorisation of distance is as follows:

- inter-urban
- up to 15km
- from15km to 30km
- from 30km to 60km
- from 60km to 120km
- over 120km.

The tariffs for the times of the day are organised as below:

● Peak hour, Monday-Friday 8.30 am - 1 pm: 150 per cent.
● Ordinary, Monday-Friday 8-8.30 am and 1-6.30 pm; Saturday 8 am - 1 pm: 100 per cent.
● Reduced, Monday-Friday 6.30-10 pm; Saturday 1-10 pm: Sunday and public holidays 8 am - 10 pm; 70 per cent.
● Economy, daily 10 pm - 8 am: 50 per cent.

You will find local telephone directories, known as **elenchi telefonici**, anywhere that has a public phone. Complete sets of telephone directories covering all of Italy's provinces are usually held by the tourist office and SIP offices. Failing that, directory enquiries can be obtained by dialing 12.

Making international calls
If you want to book an international call dial either 15 or 170. The personnel speak both French and English and operate a 24-hour service.

If you want to make a direct international call, dial 00 and then the prefix of the country to which you are making the phone call. This should be followed by the area code, but with the omission of the first '0', and then the actual telephone number. To dial London, for example, is 0044 71 and then the telephone number. A list of international prefixes is given below:

Austria	43
Belgium	32
Denmark	45
Egypt	20
Finland	358
France	33
Germany	37
Great Britain	44
Greece	30
Ireland	353
Luxembourg	352
Malta	356
Morocco	212
Netherlands	31
Norway	47
Portugal	351
Spain	34
Sweden	46
Switzerland	41
Tunisia	216
Turkey	90

Shopping in Italy

The opening hours of shops in Italy may take some time to adjust to. Generally they:

- open at 8.30 or 9 in the morning;
- close at 12.30 or 1 for lunch;
- re-open at 4.30 or 5 in the afternoon;
- close at 7.30 or 8 in the evening.

These are the standard opening hours from Monday to Saturday inclusive, all shops being closed on Sunday, except for fresh pasta shops which open on Sunday morning. While this is quite straightforward, figuring out the early closing days is more difficult. Generally speaking all shops that sell food close on a Wednesday or Thursday afternoon, although in some regions it is Tuesday. Hardware stores and shops selling appliances or machinery usually close on Saturday afternoons. Butchers often close for two afternoons in a week, usually on a Tuesday and Thursday. This should logically leave Monday as an ideal time to find all the shops open. However, Monday is frequently the closing day for places such as hairdressers, photographers, clothes boutiques and pasta shops. In the summer everybody takes a three-week holiday some time between June and October, the favourite month being August. You will find *chiuso per ferie* written on the shop doors, with the date on which it will re-open. In tourist resorts the opposite applies. Shops stay open at all hours and on all days of the week, even on national holidays, particularly if they occur during a peak tourist season.

Unlike Britain, the town centres in Italy are not dominated by faceless shopping precincts and chain stores. Supermarkets are commonplace, but they are often quite small and do not have a meat department. Most supermarkets are franchises, such as Sidis, Cral and Conad, and stock a mixture of their own and other brands as well as local produce. Small grocery stores, *alimentari*, and butchers, *macellerie*, also sell local fare and generally take pride in the quality of their products. Bakers usually bake on the premises, producing a variety of breads and rolls as well as biscuits and cakes. Patisserie and cream cakes tend to be sold in cafes. All towns also have at least one fresh pasta shop where numerous varieties of pasta are made daily.

You will be given a receipt, *ricevuta fiscale*, with all purchases, which you should keep until reaching home. The *guardia di finanza*, a branch of the police, have the right to demand to see receipts for any goods you have on you or in your vehicle, and in the unlikely event of this happening and your not having the receipt both you and the seller can be lumbered with a fine.

Some of the shops you will come across include:

alimentari	food shop/grocery
antiquario	antique dealer
calzolaio	shoe repairer
casa del formaggio	cheese shop
casa di pasta	fresh pasta shop
enoteca	wine merchant
farmacia	chemist
ferramenta	hardware store
gelateria	icecream shop
gioielleria	jeweller
macelleria	butcher
mercato	market
paneficio/panetteria	bakery
parrucchiere	hairdresser
pasticceria	cake shop
pescheria	fish shop
profumeria	perfume shop
salumeria	salami and cured meats
supermercato	supermarket
tabacchi	tobacconist
tintoria	dry cleaners
ufficio postale	post office

You will find that most towns do not have laundrettes but only dry cleaners. Some dry cleaners take in regular washing but it is an expensive habit to get into. Nearly all Italian families have a washing machine in their homes so laundrettes are only found in the biggest cities and where there is a high student or tourist population, such as in Florence.

Public Conveniences
Public conveniences come under a host of different names, including:

- *gabinetti*
- *toiletta*
- *bagno*
- *WC*.

Ladies is *signore* and Gentlemen is *signori*. You may also find the toilets labelled *donna* for women and *uomo* for men. If you cannot find a public convenience in the town, bars and cafes always have a bathroom for public use and usually do not mind you using it even if you are not a customer.

Household bills

If you are running a home in Italy you will be paying bills six times a year for your electricity, gas and telephone. There are standing charges for each of these services, so even if you are not living in your Italian home all year round you will still have bills to pay. The easiest way to pay bills is to have them directly debited from your Italian bank account. Otherwise you can pay bills at the bank or post office. To avoid the small surcharge that this incurs you may prefer to pay your bills to the appropriate local office. For the telephone go to a SIP office, for electricity find an ENEL office and for mains gas pay at the local Metano office.

Keep a record of all bills that you have paid in case you need to prove their payment at any time. You may also need to contest your bill. Electricity and gas are assessed according to an estimated consumption rather than to a meter reading. Twice a year you receive a bill, called *conguaglio*, which settles the difference between the estimated and actual consumption. This is either a nasty shock or a pleasant surprise. Should you be in credit you will receive the difference by postal order which can be cashed at the post office.

To understand exactly what is written on your bill examples for electricity, telephone and gas are shown in Figures 8, 9 and 10.

The press

Newspapers in Italy are read widely, but are not delivered to the home although they are provided in most cafes. Probably the most popular newspapers are those dedicated to sports, the gutter press restricting itself to magazines. Most of the national papers tend to be of a similar standard and format, and frequently contain a local section. Local papers also exist in their own right. In Tuscany and Umbria there is *La Nazione* and *La Gazzetta*, in Emilia Romagna there is *Il Resto del Carlino*, in the Marches there is *Il Corriere Adriatico* and in Livorno there is *Il Tirreno*. These types of papers not only provide local news but usually have pages of classified advertisements and are the place to look if you are searching for a job. Local papers, and also local editions of the national papers, usually contain emergency telephone numbers, information on entertainment and local public transport.

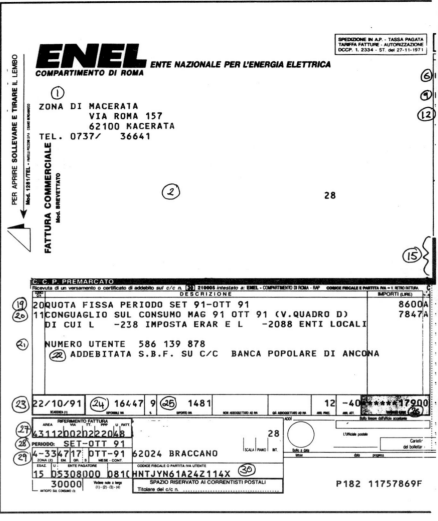

Fig. 8. Working out the electricity bill

1. Issuing office
2. Your name and address
3. Bill reference number
4. Period to which bill applies
5. ENEL reference code
6. Type of electricity supply
7. Maximum electricity power supply
8. Period being re-assessed
9. Last meter reading
10. Previous meter reading
11. Total consumption
12. Breakdown of estimated and actual consumption bi-monthly
13. Difference between estimated and actual consumption in total
14. Amount due in difference between estimated and actual consumption
15. Information regarding phoning in your meter readings

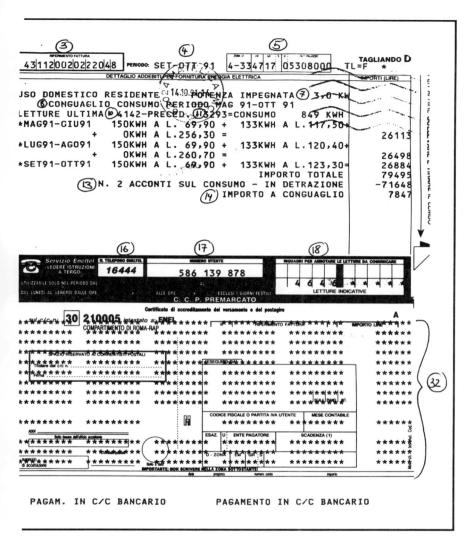

16. ENEL telephone number to use if phoning in meter reading
17. Customer number
18. Space to write down meter reading
19. Bi-monthly standing charge
20. Amount brought forward from 10
21. Customer number
22. Debit by standing order
23. Pay-by date
24. Amount subject to IVA (VAT)
25. Amount of IVA (VAT) payable

26. Total payable
27. Bill reference number (As 3)
28. As 4
29. As 5
30. Fiscal code number
31. Returnable deposit taken for connection of electricity supply
32. Information regarding the method of payment appears on this page. As this bill is paid by standing order it has been blanked out

SPEDIZIONE IN A.P. - TASSA PAGATA - TARIFFA FATTURE
AUTORIZZAZIONE DCCP - 1 / 686 / ST DEL 12 - 3 - 1969

SIP
Società Italiana per l'Esercizio
delle Telecomunicazioni p.a.

PER APRIRE SOLLEVARE E TIRARE IL LEMBO

AGENZIA DI MACERATA
VIA PIAVE,42   - 62100 MACERATA   ①

**FATTURA
COMMERCIALE**

320847739

A   737

La bolletta in dettaglio ③

UBICAZIONE IMPIANTO ④

PREF.	N. TELEFONO	BOLLETTA	SCADENZA PAGAMENTO	IMPORTO
⑤ ⑥	⑦ 6 BIM./ 92	16/11/92		27000

⑩

I PAGAMENTI DELLE BOLLETTE
PRECEDENTI SONO REGOLARI.

GRAZIE.

SCATTI EFFETTUATI DAL 1 AGOST

LETTURA AL 1 OTTOBRE ⑫
LETTURA AL 1 AGOSTO ⑬

TOTALE SCATTI EFFETTUATI ⑭

COSTO DEGLI SCATTI ⑮

N.   80 SCATTI (A L. 50) ⑯
N.   1 SCATTI (A L.127) ⑰

N.   81 SCATTI COMPLESSIVI

VEDERE SUL RETRO DELLA FATTURA IL DETTAGLIO FISCALE DEI CODICI E DELLE ALIQUOTE IVA
L'imposta di bollo, quando sia presente documento, viene assolta in modo virtuale (Aut. Int.
Fin. TO n. 36/666 ...) quando indicata il documento presente perche relativo a corrispettivi
assoggettati IVA.

ATTENZIONE: STACCARE LUNGO IL TRATTEGGIO E CONSERV

1. Issuing office
2. Customer information
3. Breakdown of the bill
4. Location of apparatus
5. Telephone code
6. Telephone number
7. Bill number (eg 6th bi-monthly bill of 92)
8. Pay-by date
9. Amount
10. Notice as to whether payments are regular or not
11. Period during which points have been assessed
12. First reading
13. Last reading

Fig. 9. Working out the phone bill

72

Mod. BREVETTATO

SI RICORDA CHE GLI UTENTI POSSONO RITIRARE LE BOLLETTE SENZA SPESE DI
SPEDIZIONE PRESSO GLI UFFICI DELL'AGENZIA SIP TERRITORIALMENTE COMPETENTE, A
PARTIRE DAL 1' GIORNO DI OGNI BIMESTRE DI FATTURAZIONE. IN TAL CASO, PER
RAGIONI TECNICHE, GLI UTENTI INTERESSATI SONO PREGATI DI DARE TEMPESTIVA
COMUNICAZIONE SCRITTA AI PREDETTI UFFICI, VALIDA FINO A REVOCA.

LA BOLLETTA PUÒ ESSERE PAGATA PRESSO LE CASSE ABILITATE DELLA SIP. GLI UFFICI POSTALI O - CON LE COMMISSIONI D'USO - PRESSO
GLI SPORTELLI DI QUALSIASI BANCA È ANCHE POSSIBILE INCARICARE LA PROPRIA BANCA DI PROVVEDERE AL PAGAMENTO DELLE
BOLLETTE IN VIA CONTINUATIVA MEDIANTE ADDEBITO SUL CONTO.

PER INFORMAZIONI RIVOLGERSI: – AL 187 (LA TELEFONATA È GRATUITA)
– ALL'UFFICIO DELLA VOSTRA ZONA (GLI INDIRIZZI SONO INDICATI NELL'AVANTIELENCO)

VENTURINI REGGIO EMILIA 9 1992

O   AL 1 OTTOBRE ⑪

1306	
1225	
81	

DETTAGLIO IMPORTI ⑲	LIRE	COD.	
COSTO SCATTI DAL 1 AGOSTO AL 1 OTTOBRE	4127	(0)	⑳
IMPIANTO BASE:CANONE BIM. NOVEMBRE-DICEMBRE	16600	(0)	㉑
ACCESSORI:CANONE BIMESTRALE NOVEMBRE-DICEMBRE	3840	(1)	㉒
SPEDIZIONE BOLLETTA	550	(0)	㉓
IVA	2645		㉔
ARROTONDAMENTO BOLLETTA PRECEDENTE	19	(2)	㉕
ARROTONDAMENTO BOLLETTA ATTUALE	-781	(2)	㉖
TOTALE BOLLETTA	27000		㉗

L. 4000	
L. 127	
PER UN TOTALE DI L. ⑱ 4127	

ARE LA FATTURA STAMPATA NEL MODULO DI VERSAMENTO.

14. Total points consumed
15. Cost of points
16. Number of points at 50 Lit. each
17. Number of points at 127 Lit. each
18. Total cost of points
19. Breakdown of costs
20. Cost of points in given period
21. Bi-monthly rent of apparatus
22. Bi-monthly rent of accessories

23. Delivery of bill
24. VAT
25. Rounding up of preceding bill
26. Rounding up of actual bill
27. Total bill

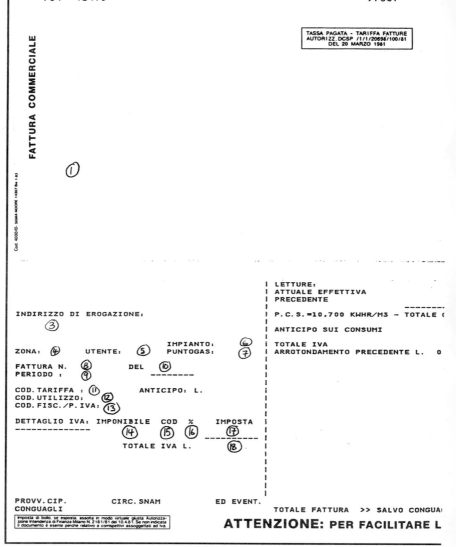

701   12175   97067

FATTURA COMMERCIALE

Cod. 4000/B- SIGMA MOORE 14307 Re. 1-93

① (1)

TASSA PAGATA - TARIFFA FATTURE
AUTORIZZ. DCSP /1/1/20698/100/81
DEL 20 MARZO 1981

I LETTURE:
I ATTUALE EFFETTIVA
I PRECEDENTE
I P.C.S. =10,700 KWHR/M3 - TOTALE (
I ANTICIPO SUI CONSUMI
I TOTALE IVA
I ARROTONDAMENTO PRECEDENTE L.   0

INDIRIZZO DI EROGAZIONE:
   ③ (3)

ZONA: ④ (4)   UTENTE: ⑤ (5)   IMPIANTO: ⑥ (6)
                                 PUNTOGAS: ⑦ (7)

FATTURA N. ⑧ (8)   DEL ⑯ (16)
PERIODO : ⑨ (9)   --------

COD.TARIFFA : ⑪ (11)   ANTICIPO: L.
COD.UTILIZZO: ⑫ (12)
COD.FISC./P.IVA: ⑬ (13)

DETTAGLIO IVA: IMPONIBILE COD % IMPOSTA
--------------   ⑭ (14)   ⑮ (15) ⑯ (16) ⑰ (17)
              TOTALE IVA L.   ⑱ (18)

PROVV.CIP.   CIRC.SNAM   ED EVENT.
CONGUAGLI   TOTALE FATTURA >> SALVO CONGUA:

Imposta di bollo, se esposta, assolta in modo virtuale giusta Autorizzazione Intendenza di Finanza Milano N. 2161/81 del 10.4.81. Se non indicata
il documento è esente perche relativo a corrispettivi assoggettati ad iva.

ATTENZIONE: PER FACILITARE L

1. Address
2. Security regulations
3. Address
4. Zone number
5. User number
6. Installation number
7. Gas point number
8. Bill number
9. Period covered by bill
10. Date from which bill is calculated
11. Tariff code
12. Code for type of use

Fig. 10. Working out the gas bill

74

NORME PER LA SICUREZZA DEGLI IMPIANTI
LA LEGGE 5 MARZO 1990 N. 46 " NORME PER LA SICUREZZA DEGLI
IMPIANTI " STABILISCE ALCUNI OBBLIGHI PER GLI UTENTI GAS :
- ESECUZIONE, MODIFICHE O AMPLIAMENTI DI IMPIANTI GAS DEVONO
  ESSERE AFFIDATI SOLAMENTE AD INSTALLATORI ABILITATI;
- L'UTENTE DEVE RICHIEDERE ALL'INSTALLATORE, A FINE LAVORI,
  UNA DICHIARAZIONE DI CONFORMITA' DELL'IMPIANTO ESEGUITO
  ALLE NORME DI LEGGE;
- ENTRO MARZO 1993 GLI IMPIANTI GAS ESISTENTI, SE NON IN
  REGOLA, DEVONO ESSERE ADEGUATI ALLE NORME DI LEGGE.
PER ULTERIORI INFORMAZIONI RIVOLGERSI AGLI UFFICI METANO
CITTA' DI ZONA.

INOLTRE COMUNICHIAMO CHE, IN APPLICAZIONE DEL PROVVEDIMENTO
C.I.P. N. 25/91, CON DECORRENZA 01/01/93, LE TARIFFE PER
RISCALDAMENTO INDIVIDUALE CON O SENZA USO PROMISCUO E PER
ALTRI USI, ESCLUSE LE TARIFFE PER USO DOMESTICO (COTTURA
CIBI E ACQUA CALDA), AUMENTANO DI LIRE 30,5 AL METRO CUBO.

PER APRIRE SOLLEVARE E TIRARE IL LEMBU →

```
DATA            GIORNI              M3
 ⑲              ⑳                   ㉑
 ㉒                                 ㉓
-------------------------------------------
CONSUMO DA FATTURARE M3:        ㉔
                      LIRE   COD
                       ㉕
                       ㉖
ATTUALE -L.    =       ㉗
```

 LIO << LIRE: ㉘   SCADENZA PAGAMENTO: ㉙

E OPERAZIONI STRAPPARE LUNGO LA PERFORAZIONE

13. Fiscal code or VAT number	21. Actual meter reading
14. Taxable amount	22. Date of preceding meter reading
15. Code	23. Preceding meter reading
16. Percentage of tax	24. Total gas consumption
17. Amount of tax due	25. Deposit on consumption
18. Total VAT	26. Total VAT
19. Date of actual meter reading	27. Rounding-up of actual and
20. Number of days between actual	preceding VAT
meter reading and preceding	28. Total bill amount
meter reading	29. Pay-by date

HOW DO I DEAL WITH RED TAPE?

Fulfilling any bureaucratic procedure in Italy is a time-consuming and often frustrating business. In the larger cities the problem is exacerbated by long queues and less than helpful staff. It is often difficult to make headway without the right personal contacts who can make things move, so many people take their problems to an agency, known as an **agenzia**, which specialises in dealing with bureaucratic formalities. As well as the correct documents almost any bureaucratic transaction requires *bolli* (state stamps), the most common type of which cost 15,000Lit. and are purchased from the *tabacchi* (tobacconists).

Police registration
Whether you are in Italy for a short-term or long-term stay you are required by law to register with the local police (either the *Questura*, or *Commissariato* or *Stazione di Carabinieri*) within three days of your arrival. If you are staying in a hotel, *pensione* or an approved campsite this formality will automatically be done for you.

Applying for a permit to stay
One of the first things you should do if you intend to stay in Italy for longer than 30 days is to apply for a *Permesso di Soggiorno* (Permit to Stay). Permits are issued by the *Ufficio Stranieri* (Foreign Department) of the Police in your regional capital, although the police in your local town may be willing to apply for the permit on your behalf. If you are applying through your local police station you will be required to write a formal letter of request accompanied by a *bollo* (state stamp). An example of the type of letter you should write is given below.

Alla Questura di (insert province)
(your name)

Il sottoscritto, nato/a (place of birth)
il (date of birth) *cittadino/a* (nationality)
in possesso di passaporto n. (passport number)
rilasciato il (date of issue) *e valido fino al* (expiry date) *rivolge corte domanda affinché gli/le venga l'autorizzazione per soggionare in Italia*, (place), *per motivi di studio/lavoro/salute* (delete as applicable).
Allega:
(make a list of enclosures)
Il/la richiedente ha fatto ingresso in Italia il (date of entry into Italy) *tramite la frontiera di* (name of frontier crossed).

recapito all' estero: (date of return)
Inoltre' dichiara di abitare a (Italian address).

Con osservanza
Firma (legible signature)

The letter should be typed on special lined paper used for legal transactions, which has wide margins at either side. It is known as **carta uso bollo** and is available from the *tabacchi* (tobacconists). Affix the correct *bolli* (state stamps) in the right-hand margin at the top of the page.

The type of permit you apply for will depend on your reason for being in Italy.

Applying for a permit for tourism

If you are staying for longer than 30 days, but not more than three months, you should apply for a **permit for tourism**. You may also need to apply for this type of permit to cover an interim period in which you may be looking for work or arranging for the transfer of money. However, at the time of writing the police do not allow a period of more than three months in order to establish a means of living in Italy.

Applying for a long-term permit

If you are staying in Italy for more than three months you will need a **long-term permit** which should be valid for five years for EC citizens. The first step in acquiring a permit is to request an application form from the Foreign Department of the Police Station. You may be asked whether you want a permit for:

● **scopo residenza** (for purpose of residence)
● **scopo dimora** (for purpose of staying), or
● **scopo lavorativo** (for purpose of work).

The next step is to complete the application form. Then return it to the police along with your passport, a photocopy of the principal pages of your passport, three passport-sized photographs, evidence of health coverage (Form E111 or private health insurance), and a *bollo* (state stamp available from a tobacconist). You may also be asked to present evidence of being able to maintain yourself, which means either a letter from an employer or a letter from your bank stating your private means.

Once you have completed this stage of the proceedings you will be asked to return at some later date to collect your permit.

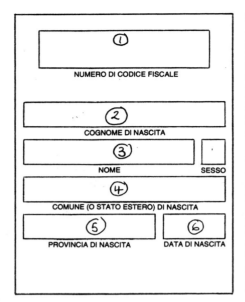
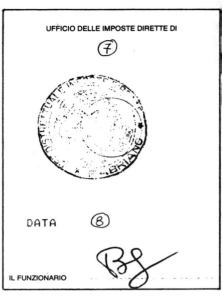

1. Fiscal code number
2. Surname
3. First name
4. Place of birth
5. Province of birth
6. Date of birth
7. Tax office
8. Date

Fig. 11. The *Codice fiscale* card

Applying for Residency

If you plan to take up residency in Italy, once you have obtained you *Permesso di Soggiorno* your next task is to register at the **Ufficio Anagrafe** (municipal registry office) in your nearest *Comune* or *Municipio* (town hall). Take your *Permesso di Soggiorno* and passport or identity card and explain that you wish to become a resident of the local *Comune*.

Once you are a resident you will find it much easier to do domestic transactions, such as opening a bank account, buying a car, having electricity connected etc, which require you to have a **Certificato di Residenza**.

To obtain this certificate simply go to the *Ufficio Anagrafe* where they will issue a print-out with the relevant information. The cost of the print-out is nominal, although most transactions require that a *bollo* is fixed to the certificate. If this is the case, buy it beforehand from the *tabacchi* (tobacconists) so that the *Ufficio Anagrafe* can put their official stamp on it.

Codice Fiscale

The **Codice Fiscale** is a card with your fiscal tax number on it. You will be asked to present this card for any number of transactions, from joining a club to opening a bank account. Registration is simple. Find out where your provincial tax office, known as **Ufficio Imposte Dirette**, is and present your passport or identity card. It will be issued there and then. Figure 11 shows an example of a *Codice Fiscale* card.

CAR AND DRIVER DOCUMENTATION

Obtaining an Italian driving licence

Foreigners resident in Italy are required by law to obtain an Italian driving licence within a year of the date on which they registered at their local *Comune* or *Municipio* (town hall). The procedure to do so is quite a lengthy one and you may prefer to avoid the whole rigmarole by buying an International Driving Licence which can be renewed each year.

However, those who want an Italian licence should read on. The first step is to have an Italian translation of your British licence made. A standard translation for a European Community-type British Driving Licence is provided below. You should transfer this translation, filling in the appropriate data, onto special lined paper with margins at either side, known as *carta uso bollo*, which is available from *tabacchi* (tobacconists). Do not write in either of the margins but in the right-hand one affix a *bollo* (state stamp), which is also available from a *tabacchi* (tobacconist).

Dipartimento di trasporto (inset country)
Patente di guida, tipo (insert type)
Nome: (insert first names)
Cognome: (insert surname)
Date e luogo di Nascita: (insert place and date of birth)
Domicilio: (insert address)
Rilasciato dal: (insert issuing office)
Il giorno: (insert date of issue)
Valido fino al (insert expiry date)
Patente (insert licence number)
Autorizzata a guidare tipo (insert code for type of vehicles authorised to drive) *soltanto I moto veicoli tipo* (insert code for authorised vehicles) *se il conducente ha l'eta per guidare. Vedere il regolamento minimo eta per guidare che e nella parte posteriore.*

A 18 anni: Motoveicoli con il massimo portata di peso non superiore a 7.5 Ton. Altri moto veicoli autorizzati di merce. Grande veicolo per passegeri in concomitanza con la regole No. 4 del motoveicoli (Licenza di guida). Regolamenti 1987. Vedere trasporto merce pesante e veicoli de trasporto pubblico. A 21 anni: Motoveicoli grandi per passegeri, con il massimo peso piu di 7.5 Ton. Altri veicoli non elencati sopra. Vedere Guida di merce pesante e Veicoli di Servizio Pubblico. I summenzionati limiti di eta non saranno applicati per i veicoli del gruppo A, B, G, H, K, L e N quando sono per uso Navale Militare ossia per motivi di Forze Aero.

Per guidare veicolo per merce pesante e veicoli di Servizio Pubblico: Devi ottenere una licenza supplementare prima di guidare sia un veicolo pesante o veicolo de servizio pubblico.

Veicolo grande per passegeri, si intende un veicolo a positamente costruito ossia trasportare piu di 9 persone compreso il conducente. Veicoli per merce: si intende un veicolo, eccetto moto veicolo grande per passegeri o pure trattori per agricoltura, costruito o adattato per trasportare tirare e con il massimo peso eccedente 3.5 Ton. Il massimo peso e il peso massimo quando il veicolo potrebbe pesare a pieno carico; comprende il peso de qualunque rimorchio o semi rimorchio. Elenco di tipo di licenze per guidare:

A. Qualunque veicoli eccetto veicoli gruppo D (Moto veicoli), tipo E (Ciclomotore), tipo G (rullo compressore), tipo H (cingolato caterpillar), tipo J (veicoli per invalidi)

E. Ciclomotore di 50CC

La sudetta patente porta un numero ad ogni margine (insert code numbers printed on edges of licence).

Once you have completed the translation you must take it to your local **Pretura** or **Tribunale** (Magistrate's Court) and have it stamped and signed by the appropriate clerk. Next you should go to the *Comune* or *Municipio* (town hall) with a *bollo* (state stamp) and three passport-sized photographs. Ask the *Ufficio Anagrafe* in your local *Comune* or *Municipio* for a *Certificato di Residenza* (Resident's Certificate) and have the *bollo* attached and stamped. Also ask someone in the *Comune* or *Municipio* to authenticate one of your photographs, verifying that it is a true likeness.

Then make arrangements for a **Certificato Medico** (Medical Certificate). First you must obtain a medical report form and an empty medical certificate. These are usually available either from an *agenzia* who deals with licence exchange (look for *patente* written in their window), or from your *Unita Sanataria Locale* (USL). Take the medical report form to your family doctor to fill in and sign. Next take the report, along with the empty medical certificate, a *bollo* and a passport-sized photograph to the *Unita Sanitaria Locale* (USL). Here you will be given an eye test, after which you will be issued with the final medical certificate.

Having done all this, gather together every single scrap of relevant paper, as well as your current driving licence, and head either to a *Motorirazzione Civile* office, the address of which can be found by looking in the *Yellow Pages* under *Ministero del Trasporto*, or delegate the task to the Automobile Club Italiano (ACI) or an *agenzia* (agent). At this stage of the proceedings you will be asked to hand over your original driving licence and a photocopy of it. It will be some days before your Italian licence is ready, therefore remember to ask for a letter or some proof that you hold a licence, in case you should be stopped by the police in the meantime. If you decide to go to the *Motorirazzione Civile* yourself, you will be asked to pay a postal order at the post office and to purchase another *bollo*. Checklist of documents for obtaining an Italian Driving Licence:

- Italian translation of British Licence with a state stamp and signature of magistrate's court
- photocopy of original driving licence
- Residence Certificate with a state stamp
- three photographs (one to be endorsed by the town hall)
- medical certificate with a state stamp.

It is necessary to affix a *Marche per Patente* (State Stamp for Licences) to your Italian driving licence every year. These are sold at the post office and also in most *tabacchi*. The cost of the stamp in 1991 was Lit.22,000, but the price increases every year, and in 1993 reached Lit.50,000. It is also necessary to renew your driving licence every ten years, which involves having an eye test done. A facsimile of an Italian driving licence is shown in Figure 12.

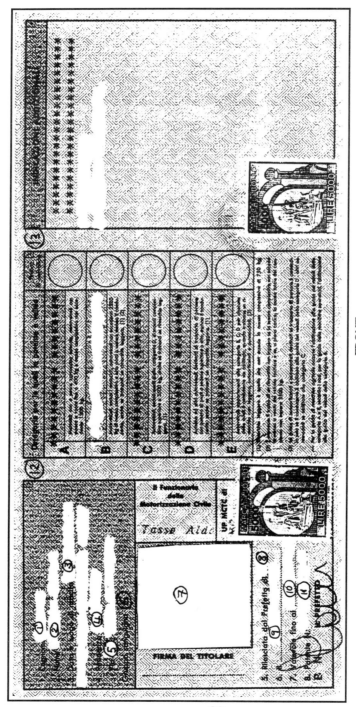

FRONT

Fig. 12. The Italian driving licence

1. Suspension of licence
2. Change of address
3. Annual authentication - official
   stamp to be affixed each year

4. Front cover
5. European Community model

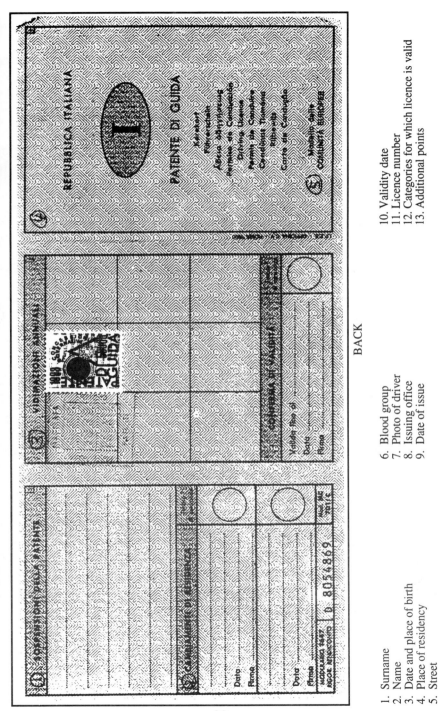

BACK

1. Surname
2. Name
3. Date and place of birth
4. Place of residency
5. Street

6. Blood group
7. Photo of driver
8. Issuing office
9. Date of issue

10. Validity date
11. Licence number
12. Categories for which licence is valid
13. Additional points

83

Importing and registering a foreign car

If you are a registered resident in Italy and have a foreign-registered vehicle you are obliged to import it and obtain Italian number plates. The procedure involved in doing this is extremely long, complicated and expensive, so if possible don't attempt it. If you have no alternative then you are well advised to use your local Automobile Club Italiano (ACI) representative to help you, although if you are living in a rural backwater you may find that the ACI office know less about the procedure than you.

The first stage in the process is to complete the importation formalities. This means that your V561 export certificate must be stamped by customs and must show any tax or duty that was paid. If you did not have this done on crossing the border you should go to your nearest customs office.

The next stage is to locate your local *Motorirazzione Civile* office, which can found by looking in the *Pagine Gialle* (Yellow Pages) under *Ministero del Trasporto*, and take along the following documents:

- V561 Export Certificate paid and stamped
- Technical Data Certificate
- authenticated translation of Technical Data Certificate
- Residence Certificate
- *Domanda in Carta Semplice*

The Residence Certificate is available from your local *Comune* or *Municipio*. The *Domanda* is a formal, typed letter on plain paper requesting the matriculation of your vehicle. A model letter is given below:

Motorirazzione Civile
Address

Date

La sottoscritto/a (name), *nato/a il* (date of birth), *a* (place and country of birth), *richiede la vista e prova per effetuare la nazionalizzazione della sua autovettura* (make and model of vehicle)
Numero Motore: (engine number)
Numero Targa: (numberplate)

in fede

(Date) (Signature)

When you present yourself to the *Motorirazzione Civile* office you will be given a form, the *Domanda di Vista e Prova per Immatricolazione* (Request for Inspection and Test for Matriculation) Model number MC2102MEC. This must be completed with all your details and the appropriate postal orders paid at a post office.

The next stage is for the *Motorirazzione Civile* to administer an inspection and test to check that your vehicle conforms to Italian standards.

Provided the vehicle passes the test you are now eligible for Italian plates. On collection of your plates you will be presented with a bill which will probably include the cost of the plates, the cost of the vehicle inspection and a fee paid to the lawyer who verified your new matriculation papers. On top of this you will pay IVA (VAT) of 19 per cent. You shouldn't be surprised by a bill in excess of 1,000,000Lit., and of course if you used an agent it will also include his fee. Your matriculation papers will be sent through the post. In the meantime you should be given a provisional document which covers you for one month.

5
Finding Accommodation

HOLIDAY ACCOMMODATION

Hotels and pensione

Italian hotels are classified under a five-star rating scheme, although the corresponding tariffs vary greatly. Prices are in general high by European standards; a single room in a one-star hotel can easily set you back 50,000Lit. However boarding houses, known as pensione, which are classified under three categories, are cheaper. Single rooms fetch between 25,000Lit. and 35,000Lit. per night. Your bill will include IVA (VAT) of 19 per cent. The state-owned fuel stations, Agip, also run a nationwide chain of motels.

If you want to book hotel accommodation before arriving in Italy you can contact a travel agent or a hotel representative. A comprehensive list of hotel representatives in the UK can be found in the *Travellers' Handbook* published by the Italian State Tourist board (see Appendix for address). However, travel agents and hotel representatives generally only deal with four- or five-star hotels. Otherwise, it is of course possible to phone a hotel directly. To book a room in an Agip Motel apply to the Head Office in Rome at:

Agip Motel Central Booking Office
Via Giorgione 63
Rome
Tel: (06) 4440183.

Holiday villages

Many Italians spend their summer vacation in a *villaggio turistico,* a holiday village, which is a self-contained complex often sited on the coast near a holiday resort, with a variety of facilities for sport and leisure as well as restaurants, shops and bars. The accommodation is self-catering, making it a very popular option for families. Bookings should be made well in advance for the months of July and August.

Agriturismo

Agriturismo is an organisation that offers vacations in rural locations, often in Italian family homes. The great majority of Agriturismo accommodation is concentrated in Trentino Alto Adige, Tuscany and Umbria, and more recently in Sardinia. The type of accommodation varies considerably, from being a very basic bed and breakfast to a plush country hotel with excursions arranged and sports facilities available. At the lower end of the range, you can expect to pay considerably less than you would for a hotel, but you may be expected to offer some work in exchange. In some Agriturismo establishments you can specify the type of lodging you want: whether it is *per nottamento e prima colazione* (bed and breakfast) or *mezza pensione* (half-board). You may find there is a special offer for a *weekend completo* (full weekend) which includes the Friday evening meal and Sunday lunch. Most Agriturismo lodgings are affiliated to a regional organisation which determines the tariffs. To find out more about Agriturismo holidays request the *Guida dell'Ospitalita Rurale* from this address:

Agriturist
Corso Vittorio Emanuele 101
Rome
Tel: (06) 6512342.

Alternatively, contact the following regional organisations:

Terra Nostra
Via XXIV Maggio 43
Rome
Tel: (06) 4682368.

Turismo Verde
Via Mariano Fortuny 20
Rome
Tel: (06) 3969931.

Associazione Agriturismo Trentino
Via Rosmini 42
Trento
Tel: (0461) 36211.

Sudtiroler Bauernbund
Perathonerstrasse 10
Bolzano
Tel: (0471) 27145.

Cooperative Allevatrici Sarde
Casella Postale 107
Oristano (Sardinia)
Tel: (0783) 4818066.

Campsites

There are some 2000 campsites dotted along Italy's coasts. They are classified into four categories and are priced accordingly, although the figures vary from district to district. Your bill will consist of a fee charged per person, a fee for the pitch, a charge for electricity, IVA (VAT) and usually a tourist tax. Children under three are generally not charged. Members of AIT ot FICC or FIA are offered discounts.

Most campsites are open from April until September or October. However, those in the mountainous northern regions do not open until June, while some sites in the warmer south stay open all year round.

For a comprehensive listing and prices of campsites in Italy contact Federcampeggio (see address below) which publishes a guide called *Campeggi e Villaggi Turistici* that is sold for approximately 30,000Lit. Federcampeggio also publishes a less costly booklet of the main campsites in Italy, all of which can be booked through an international booking centre.

Federcampeggio
Casella Postale 23
Via Vittorio Emanuele 11
Calenzano
Florence
Tel: (055) 882391.

Information on availability of space in campsites can be obtained from offices of the Automobile Club Italiano (ACI), and from provincial tourist offices known as Ente Provinciale del Turismo.

Youth Hostels

Youth Hostels are not very widespread in Italy; there are little over 50 in total and the rates often exceed those of the lowest category *pensione*. To stay at a hostel you must have a membership card issued by the International Youth Hostel Federation (IYHF). If you do not already have one it can be purchased at the youth hostel itself, an authorised travel agency, a Youth Information Centre (see Appendix for addresses) or from a centre of Associazione Italiana Alberghi per la Gioventu, the head office of which is given below:

Associazione Italiana Alberghi per la Gioventu
Via Cavour 44
Rome
Tel: (06) 462342.

WHAT LONG-TERM ACCOMMODATION IS THERE?

Doing a house exchange

Exchanging your UK home for an Italian one, either permanently or for a specified period, is a good way of solving the accommodation problem, although it is important that the conditions and securities are clearly laid out. Organisations in Italy that deal with house exchanges are:

Home Exchange International
Piazza Mirabello 1
Milan
Tel: (02) 651753.

Intervac
Via Oreglia 18
Riola
Bolzano
Tel: (051) 910818.

Casa Vacanze
Via San Francesco 170
Padova
Tel: (049) 38664.

Finding rented accommodation

Finding a place to rent is fairly difficult in most towns and cities throughout Italy. Houses are particularly hard to come by; most people rent flats. Added to the scarce availability, rents tend to be very high. To rent a two-bedroom flat in Florence, for example, costs anything from

1,500,000Lit. per month, and this is exclusive of service charges and running costs. The scarcity and high cost of rented accommodation is a direct result of a fair rent act that was passed in 1978, known as the *Legge dell 'Equo Canone'*. The act states that the minimum lease is for four years and that the rent must conform to the rates fixed by the law. The rates are calculated according to the land registry classification and the standard of the accommodation.

To find a place to rent you can:

● go to a housing agency (many agencies are only concerned with the sale and purchase of property);
● consult the local tourist office;
● look in the local papers;
● ask around locally;
● walk the streets in the area in which you plan to live looking for *affitasi* or *da affitare* (to rent) signs posted on front doors.

Once you have found a place you will have to negotiate terms, and it may be in your interest to offer to pay in undeclared cash in return for a lower rent. The landlord can ask for a deposit of up to the value of three months rent.

If you are renting a flat in an apartment block with more than five proprietors you will be liable for joint service charges. These include such things as air conditioning, cleaning services and lift maintenance and are arranged by a joint owners' assembly, known as a *condominio*. The service charges also usually encompass the cost of central heating which is run off a communal boiler. Italy has official heating times, running from October to April, which means that boilers in apartment blocks are not lit outside these times. If you wish to contest any of the service charges or facilities, the assembly will put your issue to the vote.

You may be interested to know that once you are settled in a rented flat you cannot be legally evicted except by court order. Harassment of tenants is also illegal.

BUYING A PLACE

Readers interested in purchasing a property in Italy are advised to consult the companion title in this series, *How to Rent & Buy Property in Italy*, for a detailed and practical account of the subject. The book also contains examples of the various documents you are likely to come across.

6
Health and Welfare

HOW DOES THE HEALTH SYSTEM WORK?

Public health care

The Italian public health system, the *Servizio Sanitario Nazionale* (SSN),
is administered by local health departments known as *Unita Sanitaria
Locale* (USL). There are approximately 650 USL health departments in
Italy, each of which serves between 50,000 and 200,000 inhabitants.
Depending on the size of the local population, a health department caters
for a single *comune* (commune), or an association of smaller *comuni*
(communes), or a *comunita montana* (mountain community). To locate
your local USL look in the telephone directory under *Unita Sanitaria
Locale*.

USL (pronounced 'oosle'), as well as being an administrative body,
provides public health services too. There is usually a rotation of doctors
and specialists on duty, the hours of whom can be found posted on a
bulletin board inside the building. Doctors and specialists who are *con la
mutua* (under the SSN) operate part-time *ambulatorio* (consulting rooms)
at hospitals too. There will be a noticeboard posted inside the hospital
showing the hours. Doctors and specialists who work under the SSN also
have their own surgeries, the addresses of which can be found out from
your local USL centre.

In addition, the State provides counselling, family planning and
paediatric care at local health units, known as *consultorio* (consultancy).
A *consultorio* varies from place to place, but it invariably endeavours to
serve the needs of the community in matters that are not dealt with by
USL or otherwise. To locate your local *consultorio* (consultancy) look in
the telephone directory, or if you live in a very small community enquire
at USL or your local *municipio* or *comune* (town hall).

Private health care

The private health system in Italy is well used and quite extensive, ranging from small private practices to large private hospitals. Private health care offers the obvious advantages of avoiding long waiting lists for operations, and provides the extra care and comfort that may not be available in state institutions. Italians are usually covered by *mutua* or an insurance scheme that enables them to use the private health system.

Without any such cover, the costs involved in private health care are considerable. If you use a private doctor, you can expect to pay an initial registration fee and then the cost of each visit.

Dental care

Dentists in Italy are virtually all privately run. A small and overworked number belong to the public health scheme, but they do not have a good reputation and getting an appointment can be difficult. However, private dental care in Italy is no more expensive than in the UK and treatment is generally of a high standard. It is also worth remembering that if you are making a tax declaration in Italy you can offset any dentistry receipts against your taxable income.

How do you join the public health system?

In order to be eligible for public health care in Italy you must either have form E111 (see Chapter Two) or pay the obligatory health tax, *tassa saluta*, payable annually, which provides maternity and sickness benefits as well as health assistance. If you have an Italian employer, health tax payments will probably be made on your behalf. The employer is usually responsible for paying the greater part of the contributions while the remainder is automatically deducted from the employee's salary. If you are self-employed or unemployed you must make contributions by applying to your local tax office in person.

How contributions are assessed

The contributions are assessed according to a person's salary. If husband and wife both work they are assessed separately. If there is only one wage earner in the family then their contribution will cover any dependants. Those with salaries of up to 40 million lire pay 5 per cent, while for those that earn between 40 million lire and 100 million lire, 4 per cent is deducted. If your taxable income is derived from land, property or capital the first 4 million of your income is exempt.

A problem for newcomers to the system is that the contributions are calculated according to the salary that is shown on your *denuncia* (income tax return) of the preceding year. If you have not made a tax declaration then you will be asked to pay the minimum fixed rate of 750,000Lit. In order to make this voluntary contribution you will have to present your *Attesta di Iscrizione* (Registration Card) from the *Ufficio di Collocamento* (employment office), or if you are employed you must take a statement from your employer to prove that you are working.

Registering with the SSN
All residents in Italy, even if they are temporary or only use the private health sector, are obliged to register under the SSN.

In order to register, foreign residents should take the following documents to their local USL centre:

● an official identity document
● *stato di famiglia* (family status certificate)
● *certificato di residenza* (residence certificate) (both above available from *Ufficio Anagrafe*)
● *codice fiscale* (fiscal code card)
● letter from employer stating work situation, or
● *attesta di iscrizione* (registration card) from unemployment office
● *permesso di soggiorno* (permit to stay).

If you are registering as a temporary resident then you should submit your E111 in return for a certificate of entitlement. If you do not have an E111 you may be asked to provide some document that indicates your reason for staying in Italy.

When you register you will be asked to select from an approved list a family doctor and, in the case of children under the age of 6, a paediatrician. Unless you have a personal recommendation choosing a doctor can be difficult. You may wish to consider the location of the surgery and parking availability, the opening hours, whether they speak any English and whether they have an appointment system. USL will probably not be able to answer these questions, but if you take the doctors' telephone numbers you can ring them and find out for yourself. If you find that you do not get on with your doctor you can transfer by informing USL.

After completing the registration formalities at USL you will be given a temporary cover note which lasts until your *tessera sanitaria* (health card) arrives in the post. A separate health card is issued for each member of your family. The *tessera sanitaria* (health card) is a vital document, bearing your fiscal code number, and should be carried on you whenever you need medical care. If you should lose your card then apply to USL without delay for a duplicate. The *tessera* is valid for one year only. Each time you renew it you should take all the documents that were listed for

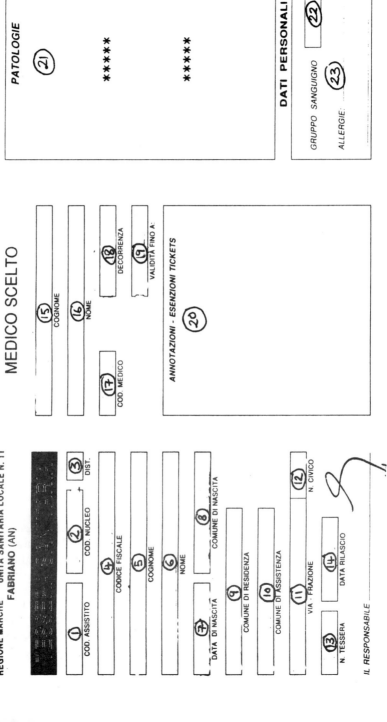

1. Assistance number
2. Unit number
3. District
4. Fiscal code number
5. Surname
6. First name
7. Date of birth
8. Place of birth
9. Municipality of residence
10. Municipality of assistance
11. Street (address)
12. Number (address)
13. Number of medical card
14. Date of issue
15. Surname of doctor
16. Name of doctor
17. Doctor's code number
18. Date valid from
19. Date valid until
20. Notes - Excemptions from tickets
21. Medical
22. Blood group
23. Allergies

Fig. 13. *Tessera sanitaria:* medical card

your initial registration as above. A facsimile of a *tessera sanitaria* is shown in Figure 13.

USING THE PUBLIC HEALTH SYSTEM

Family doctors

The touchstone in the health system, both public and private, is the family doctor with whom you enlist when you register at USL. Whether you have a dose of flu, an ingrown toe-nail, or need a medical certificate for work, your family doctor is the person to see.

The first thing to do is to find out the hours that your doctor works. Although proposals have been put forward to change the way surgeries are run, it is still generally the case that each doctor has his own small surgery which only operates for limited hours. It is seldom possible to make an appointment, surgeries usually operate on a first-come-first-served basis. Patients sort this out amongst themselves using a form of pelmanism, there generally being no secretary or receptionist. Allow plenty of time.

Inside the doctor's room there is no fear of any rigorous medical examination; pen and paper are the family doctor's instruments. The role of the family doctor is to diagnose a problem and then to write out the appropriate *impegnativa*, which is a chit that either serves to take your problem elsewhere or prescribes drugs to be purchased at the chemist. (See facsimile of *impegnativa* in Figure 14.)

Paediatricians

Italian children up to the age of 14 usually go to a paediatrician rather than the family doctor. They operate in the same way as family doctors, having their own surgeries and working within restricted hours. They write out an *impegnativa* (chit) as and when necessary, but generally problems are solved within the surgery. The paediatrician also gives routine check-ups and advises on children's diet.

What to do in emergencies

If you need medical assistance outside surgery hours go to the *pronto soccorso* (first aid) department at the nearest hospital. Alternatively, call the district duty doctor, whose number can be found in the telephone directory under *guardia medica*, or dial one of the national emergency numbers, either 112 or 113.

In tourist areas, during the holiday season, there is usually a *guardia medica turistica*, a doctor who speaks at least one foreign language. The

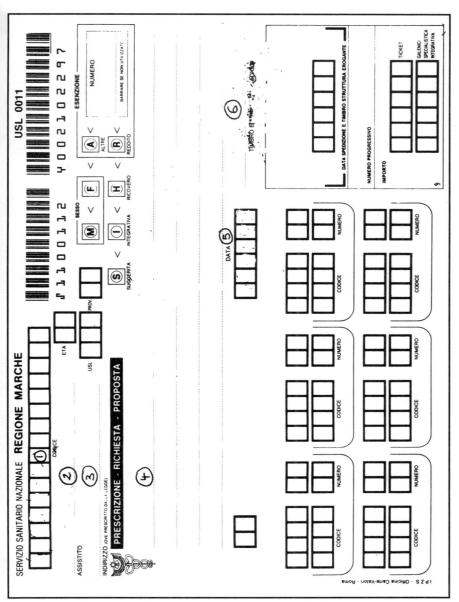

1. Fiscal Code Number
2. Name of Assisted Person
3. Address
4. Prescription - Request - Suggestion
5. Date
6. Stamp and signature of doctor

Fig. 14. A doctor's *impegnativa*

97

guardia medica turistica operates in the same way as a family doctor, as well as providing emergency assistance.

Getting medical treatment

With an *impegnativa* (chit) in hand, the next stage in the game is to get the medical attention you require. To see a specialist, who will probably work within a state hospital or an USL building, telephone beforehand to make an appointment or to find out working hours. When you arrive at the hospital or USL building hand over your *impegnativa* to the cashier and pay the *tickets*, which is the subsidised charge. In return you will be given a receipt to be taken to the relevant specialist. If your *impegnativa* is to get a laboratory test or an x-ray done, you are responsible for collecting the results and taking them back to the doctor to read. So make sure you know when and how the results are available and don't lose them!

Medical costs

If you pay state health tax you will pay subsidised charges, known as *tickets*, for specialist visits, prescribed medicines, hospital treatment, X-rays and laboratory tests. The amount of subsidy depends on your family income level. Those with incomes that do not exceed the levels as below must present a certificate, available from USL, in order to pay subsidised costs:

● one person: up to 30 million Lit.

● two people: up to 42 million Lit.

● three people: up to 50 million Lit.

For every additional person in your family add on another 5 million Lit. The members of your family include dependants as well as wage earners.

The new law enforced in March 1993 means that if your income exceeds the above levels you will pay considerably more. A flat charge of 85,000Lit. per family member is payable every year to your family doctor. You will pay the full amount for prescriptions up to 40,000Lit. and then ten per cent of any additional cost. You also pay the full cost for specialist visits and laboratory tests up to 100,000Lit. and then ten per cent of any amount in excess.

Services that are free of charge for all citizens under the SSN (National Health Service) include:

- visits to the family doctor or paediatrician;
- all treatment related to pregnancy (including abortion);
- emergency hospital treatment;
- the services at a *consultorio* (local health unit);
- emergency ambulance services (for ambulances, however, donations are usually made).

You are eligible for further health subsidies, such as exemption from the payment of *tickets*, if your family income falls below 16 million Lit. per annum. In order to find out further information consult your local USL. You will need to take proof of your income, preferably in the form of the previous year's tax declaration, or if applicable information regarding your pension or other benefit.

If you are going to make a tax declaration in Italy you should keep all receipts for medical treatment as they can be offset against your taxable income. You should also keep all medical receipts in order to make an insurance claim. This may also apply to holders of the E111 who were unable to obtain a certificate of entitlement from USL and who wish to apply for a reimbursement. Remember that medical costs include both treatment and drugs, so keep the official price tags that are attached to all medicines sold in Italian pharmacies, as well as medical bills.

HOW THE WELFARE SYSTEM WORKS

Maternity benefit

If you have been making regular INPS (welfare) contributions you should be paid maternity benefit. In order to obtain benefit apply to your local INPS office, taking with you a medical certificate confirming your pregnancy and a statement from your employer (if applicable) certifying that you have stopped work due to pregnancy. As soon as the child is born INPS expect to receive the child's birth certificate and a **stato di famiglia** (family status certificate), both of which are available from the *Ufficio Anagrafe* at your local *comune* or *municipio* (town hall).

Maternity benefit is paid for the two months preceding the expected delivery date and for the three months that follow. For women in regular employment, it is obligatory to take leave from work during this period. The benefit amounts to 80 per cent of your average daily earnings. You are also entitled to maternity benefit for six months during the year after the child is born. This allowance, however, only amounts to 30 per cent of your calculated daily earnings.

Sickness benefit

If you want to claim sickness benefit, send a medical certificate, stating the diagnosis and the period of incapacity for work, to your local INPS office. Benefit is only calculated after the INPS office receives the certificate so do not delay in its delivery. If your illness continues beyond the date indicated on the certificate, send another certificate stating that you are still ill within two days of the original one expiring.

Sickness benefit is payable for a maximum of 180 days. The amount is calculated by assessing your average daily earnings in the month preceding your illness. You can expect to receive approximately 50 per cent of this amount. If your illness lasts for more than 21 days the amount is increased to two-thirds of your average daily earnings. If you are hospitalised and do not have dependants your allowance is reduced to two-fifths of your average daily earnings.

Family allowance

If you are the sole wage earner in your family, and you work for an employer or you are a farmer, a sharecropper or a farm-hand and your salary falls below a certain level you may apply for family allowance. Submit the application form, which is available either from your employer or an INPS office, along with a *stato di famiglia* (family status certificate) from you local *comune* (town hall), to your employer. The allowance will be paid by your employer at the same time as your salary.

Pensions

All employed people, and certain categories of self-employed people such as smallholders, sharecroppers and tenant farmers, craftsmen and trades-people, are entitled to a pension from INPS. Other self-employed people who are pursuing a liberal profession, such as doctors, receive pensions through a separate organisation, the principal addresses of which are supplied below.

Ente Nazionale di Previdenza ed Assistenza Medici (ENPAM)
(National Welfare and Assistance Office for Medical Practitioners)
Via Torino 38
Rome.

Ente Nazionale de Previdenza ed Assistenza Farmacisti (ENPAF)
(National Welfare and Assistance Office for Pharmacists)
Viale Pasteur 49
Rome.

Ente Nazionale di Previdenza ed Assistenza per le Ostetriche
(ENPAO)
(National Welfare and Assistance Office for Midwives)
Lungotevere degli Inventori 88
Rome.

Cassa Nazionale di Previdenza per Gli Ingegneri ed Architetti
(National Welfare Fund for Engineers and Architects)
Via Rubicone 11
Rome.

Cassa Nazionale di Previdenza ed Assistenza a Favore dei Geometri
(National Welfare and Assistance Fund for Surveyors)
Via Cavour 178/A
Rome.

Cassa Nazionale di Previdenza ed Assistenza a Favore degli Avvocati
e dei Procuratori
(National Welfare and Assistance Fund for Solicitors and Barristers)
Via Ennio Quirino Visconti 8
Rome.

Cassa Nazionale di Previdenza ed Assistenza a Favore di Dottori
Commercialisti
(National Welfare and Assistance Fund for Economists)
Via Purificazione 31
Rome.

Cassa Nazionale di Previdenza ed Assistenza a Favore di Ragioneri e
Periti Commerciali
(National Welfare and Assistance Fund for Accountants)
Via Luigi Robecchi Brichetti 11/13
Rome.

Ente Nazionale di Previdenza ed Assistenza per i Consulenti del
Lavoro (ENPACL)
(National Welfare and Assistance Office for Employment Experts)
Viale Oceano Pacifico 44
Rome.

Cassa Nazionale Notariato
(National Fund for Notaries)
Via Flaminia 162
Rome.

Fondo di Previdenza a Favore degli Spedizionieri Doganali (FPSD)
(Welfare Fund for Customs Agents)
Via del Viminale 43
Rome.

There are two types of pension paid in Italy. The first is a *Pensione di
Anzianita*, a Seniority Pension, which is paid regardless of age provided
that you have paid contributions for at least 35 years and have ceased
working. The second is the *Pensione di Vecchiaia*, Old Age Pension,
which is obtainable at the age of 55 for women and 60 for men. If you are
self-employed the pensionable age is 60 for women and 65 for men. In
order to be eligible for an old age pension you must have paid contributions for at least 15 years. Pensions are paid on the first day of the month
preceding your application, which should be made to your local INPS
office. The amount is calculated according to the number of years in which
contributions were paid and your average earnings in the five years
preceding your pension application. The maximum pension for a worker
who has paid contributions for 40 years amounts to 80 per cent of the
highest average annual income received during the preceding five years.

Lodging an appeal

If you do not agree with a decision that has been taken regarding your
health and welfare situation you may appeal to the following institutions:

- INPS *Comitato Provinciale* (Provincial Committee)
- INPS *Comitato Speciale* (Special Committee)
- INPS *Comitato Regionale* (Regional Committee)
- *Ministero del Lavoro e della Sicurezza Sociale* (Ministry of Labour
  and Social Security).

If your appeal is not successful and you wish to take the matter further you may take your case to the ordinary courts of law.

OTHER HEALTH AND WELFARE CONCERNS

Aids

Aids is as prevalent in Italy as any other European country. There is a nationwide organisation called ANLAIDS (Associazione Nazionale Per La Lotta Contro L'Aids — National Association for the Fight Against Aids) which runs Aids prevention campaigns, diagnoses the disease and offers therapy. It also collects money for research and any donations made to it can be offset against your taxable income when you make your *denuncia* (income tax return). For further information about ANLAIDS, or indeed anything related to Aids, you will need to consult an Istituto or Clinica Universitaria per la Cura delle Malattie Infettive (Institute or University Clinic for the Cure of Infectious Diseases), or Centri per l'Assistenza alle Tossicodipendenti Gravide (Assistance Centre for Drug Addicts).

Aids information centre
To contact an Aids Centre which operates a telephone information service, dial 167861061 between 1 and 5 pm. If you are using a public telephone one token is all that is required. No charge is made when calling from a private phone.

The Aids Centre, which is located in Rome, has other phone numbers as below:

Reception: (06) 4956741
Treatment: (06) 4952761
Examination: (06) 4957242.

Drugs and alcohol

Drug abuse is widespread in Italy, perhaps not surprisingly since it is the second largest drug market in the world after the US, and drugs are comparatively cheap. However, the law is strict on prohibition and lifetime prison sentences are given to anyone found dealing in drugs.

Alcohol is less of a problem in Italy. The absence of pubs as social gathering places eliminates the beer lout, and Italian *ragazzi* (young people) tend to chat in the piazza over an ice-cream rather than an alcoholic drink. Having said this the alcohol consumption per capita is high, but this is because virtually all Italians drink wine with both lunch and dinner — and as many families have their own vineyard there are copious amounts to drink at very little cost.

The Association of Alcoholics Anonymous (Associazione Alcolisti Anonimi) has branches throughout Italy. Further information can be obtained from the head office:

Associazione Alcolisti Anonimi
Via Lupatelli 62
Roma
Tel: (06) 5280476.

Facilities for disabled travellers

Most Italian towns and cities, with their narrow cobbled streets and flights of stone stairs, are not very easily accessible to disabled travellers. Special facilities are rather few and far between. You will, however, find bathrooms for the disabled at all motorway service stations, in hospitals and usually at major tourist sights. You are well advised to plan your trip carefully, writing well in advance to the relevant tourist offices to find out exactly what facilities are available.

If you are travelling by car you must display your orange badge to use the reserved parking places that exist in most towns. If you plan to travel by train you will find that wheelchairs are taken free of charge. Special services are generally provided at airports, but it is important to specify your handicap beforehand.

For further information on travelling in Italy, contact the following address in the UK:

Radar
25 Mortimer Street
London W1M 8AB
Tel: (071) 637 5400.

Head offices of some organisations in Italy that you may wish to contact are:

Associazione Italiana Assistenza Spastici (Italian Association for Assitance to Spastics)
Via Cipro 4/H
Rome
Tel: (06) 33225057
and

Via S. Barnaba 29
Milan
Tel: (02) 5512009.

Unione Italiana dei Ciechi
(Italian Union for the Blind)
Via S. Eusebio 24
Milan
Tel: (02) 76001528.

Ente Nazionale Protezione e Assistenza Sordomuti
(National Corporation for the Protection and Assistance of the Deaf
and Dumb)
Via Gregorio VII 120
Rome
Tel: (06) 6377041.

Servizio Informazione e Valutazione Ausili
(Volunteer Assistance for the Disabled)
Via Gozzadini 7
Milan
Tel: (02) 8962253.

Federazione Italiana Sport Handicappati
(Italian Sports Federation for the Handicapped)
Viale della Tecnica 250
Rome
Tel: (06) 5921507.

Facilities for childcare

Childcare facilities for the under-3s, generally creches (known as *nido*)
are available in most towns and cities throughout Italy. Childcare facilities
at places of work are as yet undeveloped and only exist in the large,
industrial Northern cities. If you want to employ a child-minder, ask
around locally or place an advertisement in a local shop or newspaper.
You will probably find that middle-aged women who have just started to
receive a state pension are the most likely candidates. For children above
the age of 3 see Chapter Eight, page 120.

7
The Italian Job

WHAT JOB OPPORTUNITIES ARE THERE?

Employment opportunities in Italy are open to all EC citizens. However, in order to be considered for a job in Italy you must either be equal to Italian nationals in language and training, or have an exclusive ability to offer. If you work in Italy you are entitled to exactly the same terms and conditions as Italian employees. Likewise, members of your family are entitled to the same benefits as members of an Italian employee's family.

Non-EC members will find getting a job in Italy more difficult. Vacancies are only given to non-EC members if there are no Italians suitable for the job. It is also necessary to apply for an **Entry Visa for Reasons of Work** before arriving in Italy. This means that you must have a job arranged beforehand. In order to obtain a work visa send the contract with your employer's signature to the *Ufficio Provinciale del Lavoro* (Provincial Labour Office) and to the *Ufficio Stranieri* (Foreign Division) of the *Questura* (Provincial Police Headquarters). If you intend to work as a self-employed person in Italy contact the Italian Embassy or Consulate in your home country.

If you are a non-EC citizen coming to Italy for reasons other than work, but wish to take up employment after arriving, you must either be a foreign man married to an Italian woman or be a female Italian who changed nationality through marriage.

Unemployment in Italy is on the increase as recession hits industry and commerce, and more and more people lose jobs. Competition for work, therefore, is high and you should not come to Italy with false expectations. You should also remember that if by the time your temporary permit to stay has expired you have still not found a job, the police can charge you with vagrancy and escort you to the nearest border.

Looking for a job
If you are a resident in Italy and are looking for a job the first thing to do

is to report to the police station, informing them that you are seeking employment. Next go to the *Ufficio Stranieri* (Foreigners' Division) of the provincial police headquarters and apply for a three-month *Permesso di Soggiorno* (see Chapter Four) which will permit you to stay in Italy while looking for work. The next task is to obtain a *Libretto di Lavoro* (Employment Book) by taking your *Permesso di Soggiorno* (Permit to Stay) to the *Comune* or *Municipio* (town hall) where you are registered as a resident. Then take the *Libretto di Lavoro* and register at your local *Ufficio di Collocamento* (the equivalent of the Job Centre) as a job-seeker. In order to be registered in the correct category you will be asked to present copies of your qualifications, either with an official translation or a certificate of equivalence (*certificato di equipollenza* — see Chapter Two). The *Ufficio di Collocamento* will issue you with an *Attestato di Iscrizione* (Registration Card), which must be stamped regularly, and a Certificate of Unemployment. These documents are shown in Figures 15 and 16.

Go to the *Ufficio di Collocamento* regularly to see jobs that are advertised. Also look for advertisements in newspapers such as *La Repubblica, Corriera della Sera* and *La Stampa*. You could also place an advertisement yourself; Sunday is the best day. The weekly magazine *Mercatone* places advertisements for no cost and has a good section on vacancies. Other institutions you may contact for job vacancies include the *Centri di Informazione Giovani* (Youth Information Centres) (see Appendix), *Centri di Prima Accogliensa per Stranieri* (Reception Centres for Foreigners) and the trades unions, the head offices of which are:

Confederazione Generale Italiana del Lavoro (CGIL) (leftist)
Corso d'Italia 25
Rome.

Confederazione Italiana Sindacati Lavoratori (CISL) (Christian Democrats)
Via Po 21
Rome.

Unione Italiana del Lavoro (UIL) (Socialist Democrats)
Via Lucullo 6
Rome.

After finding a job

When you find a job you can apply for your three-month *Permesso di*

MODULARIO
U.L.M.O. - 53

Mod. C/15

MINISTERO DEL LAVORO E DELLA PREVIDENZA SOCIALE

Ufficio del Lavoro e della Massima Occupazione

di .... ①

_____

Comune di .... ②

Si certifica che il sig. ③ ....

....

è iscritto come disoccupato presso questo Ufficio di Col-locamento con la qualifica di .... ④ ....

al n. ⑤ .... *dal* ⑥ ....

IL DIRIGENTE L'UFFICIO DI COLLOCAMENTO

_____

- Ist. Poligr. e Zecca dello Stato - S.

1. Area unemployment office
2. Municipality
3. Name of unemployed person

4. Qualifications of unemployed person
5. Code number
6. Date on which registered unemployed

Fig. 15. Certificate of unemployment

108

Soggiorno (Permit to Stay) to be extended to the regular five-year permit. When doing this remember to take your passport or identity card and a declaration from your employer stating that you are employed. Your employer should then take responsibility for obtaining a work permit by presenting your *Permesso di Soggiorno* to the *Ispettorato del Lavoro* (Labour Inspector) who authorises a work permit. The work permit is then issued by the *Ufficio di Collocamento* (Job Centre).

Opportunities in seasonal work

If you have a job that is not expected to last more than three months you do not need to apply for a *Permesso di Soggiorno*. However, you should get a statement from your employer declaring the length of your employment.

Most opportunities for short-term employment arise during the summer months. Tourism is one of the main employers, with vacancies coming available in hotels and restaurants in the tourist resorts. To find a job, first obtain a list of hotels from the tourist office in the region of Italy in which you are interested in working. Then write a letter of application stating your date and place of birth, your work experience, your level of education, your knowledge of foreign languages, your interests, references and a photograph of yourself. Send it off early in the year.

Summer vacancies are also available in holiday villages. However, the conditions usually require someone with training in sports and other skills such as music or drama. The main vacation villages in Italy are organised by the following groups:

Club Mediterranee
Corsia dei Servi 11
Milan.

Touring Club Italiano
Corso Italia 10
Milan.

Vacanze
Via Rastrelli 2
Milan.

Valtur
Via Milano 43
Rome.

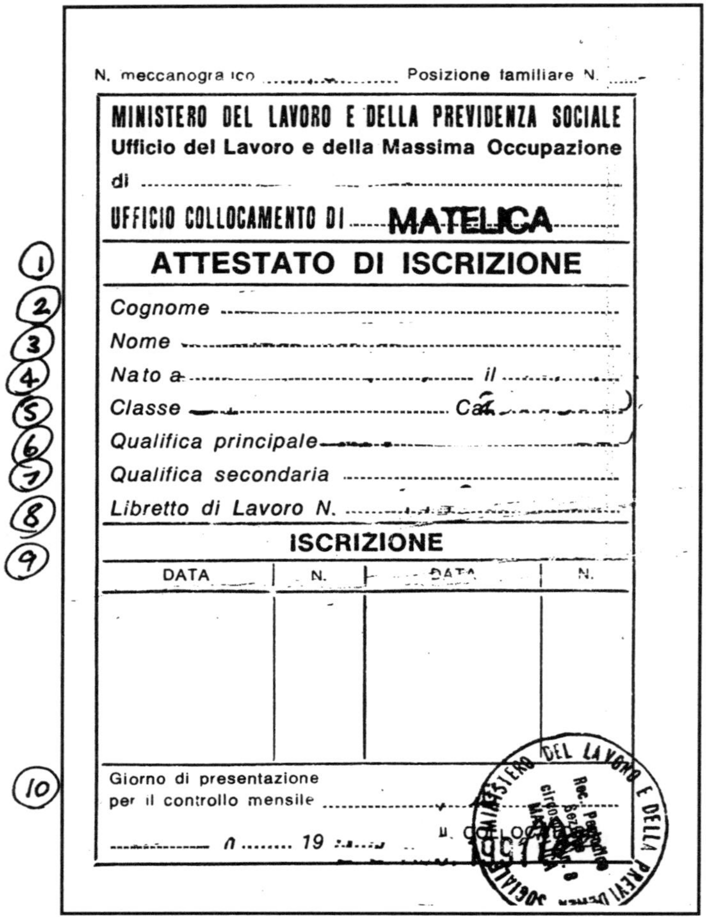

N. meccanografico .... Posizione familiare N. ......

MINISTERO DEL LAVORO E DELLA PREVIDENZA SOCIALE
Ufficio del Lavoro e della Massima Occupazione
di ....

UFFICIO COLLOCAMENTO DI ...MATELICA...

ATTESTATO DI ISCRIZIONE

Cognome ....
Nome ....
Nato a .... il ....
Classe .... Cat. ....
Qualifica principale ....
Qualifica secondaria ....
Libretto di Lavoro N. ....

ISCRIZIONE

DATA	N.	DATA	N.

Giorno di presentazione
per il controllo mensile ....
.... li .... 19 ......   IL COLLOCATORE

1. Certificate of inscription
2. Surname
3. Name
4. Place of birth and date of birth
5. Classification and category of unemployment
6. Principal qualification
7. Secondary qualification
8. Work book number
9. Inscription date and number
10. Day on which to present yourself for monthly control

Fig. 16. Unemployment registration card.

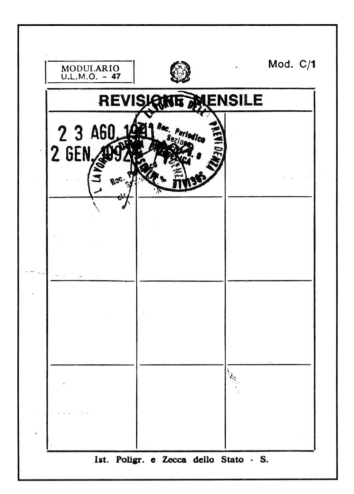

The back of the card as shown here is where the unemployment office put their stamp each time you go for a monthly control (see 10)

During harvest time you may be able to find temporary work on a farm. To find out addresses of farms and agricultural cooperatives where you can apply for work, contact the *Centri Informazione Giovani* (Youth Information Centres) (see Appendix) in the region you are interested in. The main harvests take place as follows, although you should note that there is no great recruitment of foreign workers as in some Mediterranean countries.

- May-August: strawberries, cherries, peaches and plums in Emila Romagna;
- September-October: apples and pears in Emilia Romagna, Piedmont and Trentino;
- September-October: grapes in Emilia Romagna, Lazio, Piedmont, Puglia, Trentino, Veneto, Tuscany and Marches;
- November-December: olives in Puglia, Trentino, Veneto, Tuscany, Marches, Liguria, Calabria and Sicily;
- November-December: flowers in Liguria, Tuscany, Lazio and Puglia;
- November-December: tobacco in Umbria, Puglia and Campania.

Aupair work

The best way of finding aupair work in Italy is to contact a reputable agency in the UK. The conditions associated with aupairing are clearly stated by the Provincial Labour Office in Italy and stipulate that:

- the worker shall not be under 17 years old or over 30 years of age;
- the worker shall be guaranteed health and social insurance cover;
- the worker shall be given board and lodgings as well as a sum of money for personal expenses;
- working hours must allow at least one day off a week (apart from Sunday) and also time to attend language, cultural or vocational advancement courses.

A person intending to be employed as an aupair must send one of the three copies of the 'Aupair Contract', along with a medical certificate that has been issued within the three previous months, to the local Provincial Labour Office. This office authorises a stay of one year, which is thereafter renewable for another year. This authorisation must then be submitted to the police who will issue a Permit for Aupair Employment. Alternatively, ask your host family to accompany you to the provincial police headquarters to inform them that you are a guest and that the purpose of your stay is to learn Italian and not to work.

If all this sounds laborious, it is, and you will probably find that most families simply do not bother, particularly as they are loath to pay the health insurance contributions. If this is the case all well and good, but remember that you will be responsible for your own health insurance. To complicate the scene still further British citizens should note that the UK is not a signatory to the European agreement on aupair placement. In theory this means that British citizens cannot be employed as aupairs in Italy. You will therefore be described as a nanny, mother's help or domestic help, etc, in order to avoid the problem. For further information on the conditions of aupair work contact the following organisation:

Attivita e Relazione Culturali con L'Estero
Via Garibaldi 20/1
Genoa
Tel: (010) 200481.

English language teaching

There is a big demand in all the major Northern Italian cities for English language teachers. Private language schools tend to have a fast turnover of teachers and so vacancies are regularly available. Vacancies are also to be had within the state education system, although these posts are more difficult to come by and generally less well paid. The system for applying for a teaching job, either in the state or private sectors, is to write a *domanda*, a letter of request. Your letter should include a curriculum vitae and a photograph of yourself, and should state the dates from which you are available for work. If you are already living in Italy you should look out for the **ordinanza**, a decree by which you can enrol yourself onto a teaching register. The *ordinanza* appears in the newspapers and is circulated around schools once every two years. The resulting register, known as the **graduatoria**, is then used by schools in order to fill vacancies. Teachers who are listed on the *graduatoria* have precedence over teachers who make private applications to a school.

Teaching jobs in private language schools tend to be paid by the hour, while state schools pay a salary per month. The state is renowned for the tardy payment of its salaries — be warned! However, a job in a state school is the more secure option as your contract will probably ensure that health and pension contributions are paid on your behalf. If you are employed on a full-time basis, you will be paid the equivalent of 13 months per annum, the month of December being paid double. Contracts with private language schools generally do not involve the payment of health and pension contributions. You will simply have the 19 per cent IRPEF income tax, which is equivalent of PAYE, deducted each month. Since wages in private language schools are calculated by the hour you should find out whether there are a guaranteed number of working hours, and the policy on being paid for students who book a lesson but do not attend.

Self-employment

The self-employed in Italy are categorised as *indipendente* (independent) and fall under different social security legislation from those that are *dipendente* (dependent). If you are setting up your own business in Italy one of the first things you will want to do is to find a reliable *commercialista* (book-keeper). A *commercialista*, apart from keeping accounts and making tax returns, may also handle the bureaucracy which is involved in opening a company. The cost of employing a *commercialista*, however, may be something you wish to avoid. In that case, one of the first steps to take in opening a company is to locate your provincial *Camera di Commercio* (Chamber of Commerce) which will provide information on how to establish your business. You will also need to register at the *Camera di Commercio* (Chamber of Commerce) to obtain a *certificato di iscrizione della Camera di Commercio* (certificate of registration at the Chamber of Commerce).

Should I register for IVA (VAT)?

At the same time as the procedures above you should make an application to register for **IVA** (VAT). To do this go to the provincial *Ufficio IVA* (VAT Office) and request an application form AA9/5. There is a fixed annual charge to be registered with IVA as well as other taxes, including the new minimum tax that was introduced in 1993 and which all IVA-registered people are obliged to pay. Being IVA-registered also means that you are obliged to pay into the INPS social security and pension scheme. Before rushing ahead and becoming registered make sure that you have enough VAT bills to offset the costs and note that IVA on fuel is only reimbursed to travelling salespersons and representatives. Once you hold the *partita IVA* (VAT registration number) you will be given a *libretto* (booklet) in which to record your bills.

Joining the Professional Register

All private businesses are necessarily classified and registered in an *Albo Professionale* (Professional Register). In order to be entered onto this register you must meet the qualifications required by the Chamber of Commerce. You may find that you have to sit a routine examination. Some of the main classifications of professional people are given below.

- libera professionista (professional man/woman)
- avocati (lawyers)
- commercialisti (accountants)
- medici (medics)
- artigiani (craftsmen)
- commercianti (traders)
- agricolturi (agriculturists).

Other documentation
If you are establishing a commercial enterprise you must apply for an *Atto Costitutivo della Societa Omologato dal Tribunale* (memorandum and articles of association ratified by the tribunal). All documents that you obtain during the establishment of your business should be taken to the *Questura* (police headquarters) when you come to renew your *Permesso di Soggiorno*.

MONEY MATTERS

What should be in my contract?
When you sign a work contract, *contratto di lavoro*, check that it indicates the salary and form of payment, the working hours and holidays, the length of the contract and also that it gives a definition of the work and how it should be done. In addition, a contract should state how social security contributions are to be paid. Two-thirds of contributions are normally paid by the employer, the remainder being deducted at source from the employee's salary. A typical contract may state that 24 per cent of your salary is contributed by your employer while 9 per cent of your earnings are deducted at source. Social security contributions should cover health assistance, sickness benefit and provide an old-age pension. You should also make sure that you are covered by insurance against accidents at work and occupational diseases. The body responsible for this is INAIL *Istituto Nazionale per l'Assicurazione Contro gli Infortuni sul Lavoro* (National Institution for Insurance Against Accidents at Work). Contracts can only be legally given to people aged 18 or over. However, 16-18 year olds can enter into contracts provided that they are married or are living independently with the consent of a legal guardian.

Income tax
The Italian taxation system, designed to confound the most cunning tax evaders of which Italy has more than its fair share, has, until recently, been fairly unsuccessful. The system is becoming more foolproof now with all

information stored on computers, although there are still those who continue to find loopholes, placing ever heavier burdens on the honest tax payer.

The three basic types of income tax are:

● *IRPEF (Imposte sui Reditti delle Persone Fisiche)* which is Personal Income Tax;

● *IRPEG (Imposte sui Reditti delle Persone Giuridice)* which is Corporate Income Tax, only paid by businesses involved in commerce;

● *ILOR (Imposte Locale Sui Reditti)*, Local Income Tax.

IRPEF is the tax that affects everybody. It operates in the same way as PAYE in Britain, being regularly deducted. The IRPEF payments are made every month, either by yourself or by your employer at the local tax office. Each time a tax contribution is made be sure to get an official receipt, *attestato di versamento*, (see Figure 17). Official receipts are used to settle your final tax bill in your annual *denuncia*, tax return.

On your tax return the amount of IRPEF that is due depends on your salary. It works on a sliding scale, which was in 1992:

	under	7,200,000Lit.	10%
7,200,000Lit.	–	14,400,000Lit.	22%
14,400,000Lit.	–	30,000,000Lit.	27%
30,000,000Lit.	–	60,000,000Lit.	34%
60,000,000Lit.	–	150,000,000Lit.	41%
150,000,000Lit.	–	300,000,000Lit.	46%
	over	300,000,000Lit.	51%

Fixed sums that can be offset against your taxable income are:

● wife   675,000Lit.
● child   78,000Lit.
● other family   108,000Lit.
● subordinate income   648,000Lit. (provided that your annual income does not exceed 12,400,000Lit.)

Other costs that can be offset against your tax bill include:

● mortgages

- medical bills
- donations to the Third World
- donations to the church (up to 2 million)
- personal insurance premiums (up to 21/2 million)
- divorce proceedings
- funeral expenses (up to 1 million)

If the final outcome of your tax return is that you have paid too much tax then you must request a refund. This is usually done through your local bank by requesting an *accreditamento dei rimborsi IRPEF*. The reimbursement will be paid into your bank account within two to three years.

If you work for an Italian employer you will be taxed at source and you will probably find that your tax return is taken care of. Otherwise it is your responsibility to file a tax return every May or June. The tax return, or *denuncia* as it is known, is difficult to complete even for Italians. You are therefore well advised to employ an *agenzia* (agent), a *Consulente di Lavoro* (work consultant) or a *Commercialista* (accountant). If you are really in trouble you should go to an *Ufficio di Consulenza Fiscale*, a tax consultancy office. Before approaching a professional make sure you have all relevant documents assembled. These include *buste* (pay-slips), *attestati di versamento* receipts for the payment of any tax you have paid during the year (see facsimile Figure 17), receipts for medical treatment, dental care, donations to charity and any other costs that can be offset against your taxable income. You should also purchase the correct *modulo* (form) on which the tax return is made, either 740 or 101. The *modulo* (form) is sold at *tabacchi* (tobacconists) from the end of April to the end of May.

Unemployment benefit

Unemployment benefit in Italy is virtually non-existent. The ordinary allowance, *indennita ordinaria*, is a very meagre sum, amounting to 800Lit. per day. It is paid to people who lose their jobs, and who have paid INPS contributions for at least two preceding years. If you have made contributions in another EC country, these will be taken into account. The allowance is only payable for up to six months.

A special allowance, *trattamenti speciali*, is awarded to dismissed workers in the construction industry and agriculture. The allowance is calculated as a percentage of earnings. In very exceptional cases an extraordinary allowance is granted, the *sussido straordinario*. It is granted to people who are not eligible for the ordinary allowance and who live in specific areas.

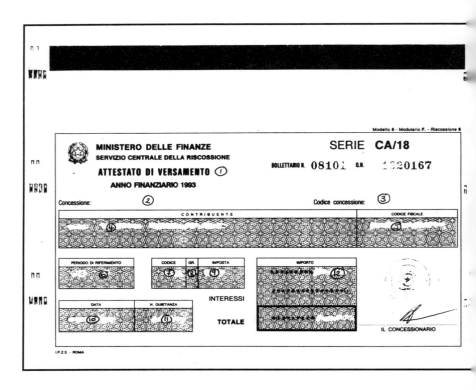

1. Certificate of payment
2. Concession
3. Concession code
4. Tax payer
5. Fiscal code number of tax payer
6. Period of reference
7. Code
8. Grade
9. Tax
10. Date
11. Receipt number
12. Amount

Fig. 17. Receipt of tax payment

To apply for unemployment benefit you must present your notice of dismissal either to your local INPS office or to the *Ufficio di Collocamento* (Job Centre), along with a *Stato di Famiglia*, a certificate from your local *Comune* or *Municipio* that indicates the status of your family.

Casual workers, performing artists in the cinema or theatre, workers whose remuneration consists of a share of the profits of an undertaking, and workers whose occupation provides work for less than six months are not normally covered by unemployment insurance. Likewise, those who have never had a job will have great difficulty in claiming unemployment benefit.

8

The Italian Education System

WHAT SCHOOLS ARE AVAILABLE?

Schools under the Italian State system are free to all dependents of residents of Italy, regardless of nationality, from the age of 3 until 19. Education is compulsory from age 6 to 14. All school education, both within the private and public sectors, is controlled by the state and conforms to the curriculum laid down by the *Ministero della Pubblica Istruzione* (Ministry of Public Education). The management and administration of schools are locally organised, with district school councils and provincial school councils composed of teachers, parents, students and representatives of social and cultural bodies. A certain amount of local autonomy is also permitted within the structure of experimental courses that are held at secondary level. Generally speaking you will find that education is at a considerably higher standard in the North of Italy than in the South.

The school year runs from mid-September to mid-June. Classes are generally held in the mornings only, but there are school six days a week. From primary level upwards, students are expected to spend their afternoons doing homework and private study.

Low-achieving children and those with minor handicaps are integrated in normal classes, but usually have a special teacher who dedicates extra time within the class.

Nursery school

The state provides at least one *Scuola Materna* (Nursery school) in every Italian town for children aged from 3 to 6 years old. As it is not obligatory, it is generally attended by children with working parents. The doors open at 8 am and usually close at 5.30 with lunch provided at a daily charge. Waiting lists for nursery schools can be for two or three years so make sure you register within plenty of time. There are also numerous private nursery schools, some of which are run by Catholic organisations. Around

Rome and the cities of Northern Italy you will find a number of private nursery schools that are conducted in English. However, you can expect to pay considerable fees.

Elementary school

Scuola Elementare (Elementary school) is from the age of 6 to 10 years old. The school day is four hours long, during which time children are under continual assessment of both their personality and behaviour as well as their educational achievements, all of which is recorded on *schede* (personal cards). If the required achievements are not reached pupils do not graduate from one year to the next, but repeat the year. On completion of the elementary school an examination is set in order to graduate to middle school.

Middle school

Scuola Media (middle school) education is for children from the age of 11 to 14. The school day is of five or six hours duration. Assessment is based on an annual evaluation by the class teacher who writes a report on the student's behaviour, attitudes, tendencies and level of achievement. At the end of the three years an examination is taken in order to graduate to upper secondary school.

Upper secondary school

Scuola Secondaria di II Grado (upper secondary school), which is not obligatory, is for students aged from 15 to 19 years. There are five basic types of secondary school:

● Liceo Classico (Classics Lyceum)

● Liceo Scientifico (Scientific Lyceum)

● Liceo Artistico (Artistic Lyceum)

● Istituto Tecnico (Technical Institute)

● Istituto Professionale (Vocational Institute).

The Classics and Scientific schools tend to be attended by students who intend to go on to university. The Technical and Vocational Institutes tend to lead directly to specific careers.

English-speaking schools

International schools and other private schools hold tuition in English, and

are run by British and American teachers and administrators. Below is a
list of the principal English-speaking schools in Italy.

Ambrit International School
Via Annia Regilla 60
Rome
Tel: (06) 7182907.
(age range 3-13 years).

American Overseas School of Rome
Via Cassia 811
Rome
Tel: (06) 3664841
(age range 4-18 years).

Castelli International School
Via degli Scozzesi 13
Grottaferrata
Rome
Tel: (06) 9459977
(age range 5-14 years).

'Core': The Co-Operative School
Via Orvino 20
Rome
Tel: (06) 8392873
(age range 3-11 years).

The International Academy
Via di Grottarossa 295
Via Cassia 10km
Rome
Tel: (06) 3666071
(age range 2-14 years).

Kendale Primary International School
Via Gradoli 86
Tomba di Nerone
Rome
Tel: (06) 3667608
(age range 3-11 years).

Marymount International School
Via di Villa Lauchli 180
Rome
Tel: (06) 329 0671
(age range 3-18 years).

St George's English School
Via Cassia km16
Rome
Tel: (06) 3790141
(age range 3-18 years).

St Stephen's School
Via Aventina 3
Rome
Tel: (06) 5750605
(age range 13-19).

Southlands English School
Via Teleclide 20 (Via Epaminonda)
Casal Palocco
Rome
Tel: (06) 6090932.

The International School of Milan
Lower Schools
Via Caccialepori 22
Milan
Tel: (02) 4073663
(age range 3-11).

The International School of Milan
Upper Schools
Via Bezzola 6
Milan
Tel: (02) 4524748
(age range 12-19).

The Amity School
Via dei Cappuccini 5
Arezzo
Tel: (0575) 300893
(age range grade 7-12).

English International School
Via Adria 4
Padua
Tel: (049) 8804190
(age range — primary level).

Vicenza International School
Stradella Moro 57
Vicenza
Tel: (0444) 500177
(age range 12-18 years).

American International School of Florence
Villa Le Tavernule
Via del Carota 16
Bagno a Ripoli
Florence
Tel: (055) 640033.

International School
Strada Costiera 11
Trieste
Tel: (040) 3787440.

Collegio del Mondo Unito dell'Adriatico
Via Trieste 29
Duino
(age range 16-18 [for Baccalaureate Certificate]).

FURTHER EDUCATION

University
The universities of Rome, Naples, Milan, Bologna and Turin account for half the university population of Italy. There are, however, 41 universities in total, all of which are run by the State. In addition there are four officially recognised private universities, two polytechnics, three special institutions of higher education, eight university institutes of education and 21 higher institutes of physical education. There are also two schools of Italian language and culture, namely the Universita Italiana per Stranieri di Perugia and the Scuola di Lingua e Cultura Italiana per Stranieri di Siena.

A foreign student in Italy can take university courses at the following levels

- *Diplomi Universitari*
- *Scuole Dirette a Fini Speciali*
- *Laurea*

The first two involve two- to three-year courses leading to a diploma. The *Corsi di Laurea*, which are for four or five years, or in the case of Medicine 6 years, are courses leading to the *Laurea* diploma and the title *Dottore* (doctor). *Post Lauream*, specialised courses and research doctorates also exist.

The university system is organised so that anybody who has attended secondary school has the right to go to university. There are no interviews and no qualification specifications (apart from secondary school diploma). As a result the popular courses are excessively overcrowded, but due to the rigour and expense of university education drop-out numbers are amongst the highest in Europe.

The negative aspects of university in Italy include the high cost of accommodation and the limited availability of halls of residence, or any other subsidised student housing. For this reason, most Italian students go to the university in their home town or as close by as possible so that they can continue living at home. The accommodation problem is exacerbated when students fail to pass their annual examinations and so have to repeat the year. The good news is that there are no tuition fees as such, instead there are annual taxes that are paid on registration. It is necessary to complete the registration procedure every year when taxes are updated. The tax varies from faculty to faculty; first year enrollments range from 350,000Lit. to 500,000Lit.

Information for foreigners wishing to attend Italian university can be obtained by writing to the relevant university and requesting the *Guida per lo Studente Straniero* (Guide for the Foreign Student).

Study grants

Grants are awarded to Italian students whose family's income falls within a certain bracket. If you are an EC citizen with family resident in Italy you have the same rights as Italian nationals to apply for a university grant. The first step in applying for a grant is to contact the *Ente per il Diritto allo Studio Universitario* at the university or education institute of your choice. Grants are not administered on a national level and so the amount of benefit you receive varies from place to place.

If you are a foreign student whose parents are not resident in Italy you are unlikely to be awarded an Italian grant but you may apply for financial aid from an international body. One way of finding out information about grant-giving bodies is to consult the Noopolis Data Bank, a non-profit making organisation that continuously updates its data on grants and scholarships. The databank can be consulted at all Italian universities as well as some student welfare offices and youth information offices (see Appendix). For further information on the databank write with your personal details to the Noopolis head office:

Via Domenico Tardini 33
Rome
Tel: (06) 6633103.

An annual sum of money is also allocated to foreign students wishing to attend Italian university, by the Italian Ministry of Foreign Affairs. For further information contact the Ministry at the address below, or consult an Italian Cultural Institute abroad (see Appendix for addresses).

Italian Ministry for Foreign Affairs
Direzione Generale Relazioni Culturali
Ufficio VI
Piazzale Farnesina 1
Rome
Tel: (06) 36911.

The Erasmus Programme, which is funded by the European Commission, is another organisation you might wish to apply to for financial support. It offers scholarships and loans to university students who wish to complete a part of their studies in Italy (or any other EC country). For further information on Erasmus contact:

Erasmus Bureau
Rue d'Arlon 15
B-1040 Brussels
Tel: (02) 2330111.

The national agency for the administration of Erasmus scholarships in Italy is as follows:

Direzione Istruzione Universitaria
Erasmus
Ministero della Pubblica Istruzione
Viale Trastevere 76
Rome
Tel: (06) 58491.

The national agency in Britain for Erasmus is:

UK Erasmus
Student Grants Council
The University
Canterbury CT2 7PD
Tel: (0227) 762712.

Otherwise you may wish to support yourself by taking up a part-time job. Note, however, that as a student at an Italian university it is against the law to work for more than 500 hours per year.

Applying for Italian university

Foreign students wishing to attend an Italian university should apply through the Italian Consulate in their home country in January. The Consulate will send a list of the required documents and an application form on which you are to select four universities, placing them in order of preference. On receipt of the application the Consulate will send EC citizens an identity card that is stamped with a consul's visa, while non-EC citizens are issued with a student visa. These documents are to be presented to the *Questura* (Police Headquarters) within eight days of arriving in Italy, in order to receive a *Permesso di Soggiorno* (Permit to Stay).

Foreign students whose parents, sisters, brothers or spouse are resident in Italy should apply by addressing themselves in person to the university of their choice. You will be asked to submit a formal application bearing the correct denomination of *bolli* (state stamps). In addition you should enclose your original educational certificates, birth certificate, recent photographs and receipt of payment of registration tax.

Foreign students are also expected to sit an Italian language examination before being admitted. If the exam is failed then foreign students who have applied for university from overseas are obliged to return to their home country.

ITALIAN COURSES FOR FOREIGNERS

Italian language and culture courses

There are a good number of Italian language and culture courses for foreign students held in Italian universities as well as at private schools. The courses generally range from two to 12 weeks duration, with food and accommodation available at an additional cost. Language courses are held at all levels and the courses on Italian culture cover a wide spectrum of subjects ranging from Etruscan History to Contemporary Italian Literature. Florence has the greatest concentration of courses on offer with around 25 private language schools in operation. Perhaps the widest ranging courses are offered by the Universita Italiana per Stranieri, in Perugia, and the Scuola di Lingua e Cultura per Stranieri in Siena, both of which are funded by the State. It is possible to apply for grants to attend either of these schools. The grants are funded by the schools themselves and also by the *Ministero degli Affari Esteri* (Italian Ministry for Foreign Affairs). To find out more about grants apply to your local Italian Consulate or Italian Cultural Institute (see Appendix for addresses).

Attending an Italian course at either of the above schools or in a university is generally less expensive than enrolling at a private school. The disadvantage of language courses at universities is that they are often only held during the summer, and not all year round, as they are in private schools or at the state schools in Perugia and Siena.

The addresses for the schools in Perugia and Siena are given below, as are the addresses of Italian universities that hold Italian language courses. Request the annual programme for further information and the cost of registration fees and accommodation.

Universita Italiana per Stranieri
Palazzo Gallenga
Piazza Fortebraccio 4
Perugia
Tel: (075) 64344.

Scuola di Lingua e Cultura Italiana Per Stranieri
Piazza Grassi
Siena
Tel: (0577) 49260.

Centro di Cultura per Stranieri
Universita degli Studi di Firenze
Via Vittorio Emanuele 64
Florence
Tel: (055) 472139.

Centro Internazionale di Studi Italiani
Universita degli Studi di Genova
Via Balbi 5
Genoa
Tel: (010) 2099868.

Corsi Internazionali di Lingua e Cultura Italiana
Universita degli Studi di Milano
Via Festa del Perdono 7
Milan

Centro Linguistico di Ateneo
Universita degli Studi di Parma
Viale delle Scienze
Parma
Tel: (0521) 580570.

Centro Interfacolta per L'Apprendimento delle Lingue
Universita degli Studi di Trento
Via Bomporto
Palazzetto CTE
Trento
Tel: (0461) 881411.

Universita degli Studi di Urbino
Via Saffi 2
Urbino
Tel: (0722) 305226.

Centro Linguistico Interfacolta
Universita degli Studi di Venezia
Santa Croce 2161
Venice
Tel: (041) 5241642.

Ente Regionale per la Gestione del Diritto allo Studio Universitario
Via San Cristoforo 4
Verona
Tel: (045) 597144.

Other courses for foreigners

There is a selection of private courses designed for foreign students, ranging from art restoration to tourism and marketing. The courses last from two weeks to one year. Contact the following addresses for further information.

Accademia del Diletto Principessa Elena
Sul Prato 58
Florence
Tel: (055) 282831
(art).

Istituto Internazionale di Scienze Turistiche
Via Torta 9
Florence
Tel: (055) 2396146.
(tourism).

Istituto per l'Arte e il Restauro
Palazzo Spinelli
Borgo Santa Croce 10
Florence
Tel: (055) 244808
(art and restoration).

Scuola di Animazione Turistica e del Tempo Libero
Borgo degli Albizi 54
Florence
Tel: (055) 2477933
(tourism).

Scuola di Architettura del Giardino e del Paesaggio
Villa Montalto
Via del Salviatino 6
Florence
Tel: (055) 613634
(architecture and landscape gardening).

Scuola di Grafica e Arredamento
Via Maggio 13
Florence
Tel: (055) 282951
(graphics and interior design).

Scuola di Marketing e Tecniche di Comunicazione
Via del Salviatino 6
Florence
Tel: (055) 613634
(marketing and communication).

Scuola di Oreficeria
Via Maggio 13
Florence
Tel: (055) 282951.
(jewellery).

Scuola per Interpreti Turistici
Via Torta 9
Florence
Tel: (055) 2396146
(interpretor).

Scuola Superiore di Arti Sceniche di Firenze
Borgo degli Albizzi 54 rosso
Florence
Tel: (055) 2477933
(drama).

Scuola Superiore per la Moda
Borgo Santa Croce 10
Florence
Tel: (055) 2345898
(fashion).

The International School of Art and Humanities
Via Sant Egidio 12
Florence
Tel: (055) 2345802.

Centro Pontevecchio
Gaiole in Chianti
Siena
Tel: (055) 294511
(cookery, gardening, language, painting).

Istituto Italiano Arte Artigianato e Restauro
Viale di Porta Ardeatina 108
Rome
Tel: (06) 5757185
(crafts and restoration).

THE CASE OF THE ITALIAN STUDENT

Carla, an Italian student after 5 years of studying political science (doesn't everyone?) was told that she would have to sit an English examination. She received no preparation for it on her course and when she took it, failed. But there again so did all one hundred and eighteen other students on her course. Two passed! Carla took private English lessons for 6 months, only to fail again as the examination format had been changed without her being informed. After 6 more months of private lessons she was ready to take it again but had to hang around the university for over a week as no date had been announced and it could be any minute. Finally she did take the exam, and passed, and so completed her degree.

Moral: never give up but avoid the higher education system if at all possible! It isn't run for the benefit of the students!

Appendix of Further Information

USEFUL ADDRESSES ABROAD AND UK

Italian Cultural Institutes

Italian Cultural Institute
39 Belgrave Square
London SW1X 8NT
UK
Tel: (071) 235 1461.

Italian Cultural Institute
82 Nicholson Street
Edinburgh EH3 7HW
UK.

British Italian Society
172 Regent Street
5th Floor
London W1
UK

British Italian Society
24 Rutland Gate
London SW7 1BB
UK
Tel: (071) 823 9204.

Italian Cultural Institute
Fitzwilliam Square 11
Dublin
Eire.

Italian Cultural Institute
1601 Fuller Street NW
Washington DC 20009
USA.

Italian Cultural Institute
686 Park Avenue
New York NY 10021
USA.

Italian Cultural Institute
500 North Michigan Avenue
Suite 530
Chicago IL 60611
USA.

Italian Cultural Institute
225 Bush Street No 310
San Francisco
CA 94108
USA.

Italian Cultural Institute
12400 Wilshire Boulevard
Suite 310
Los Angeles
CA 90025
USA.

Italian Cultural Institute
275 Slater Street
Ottawa KIP 5IP
Canada.

Italian Cultural Institute
1200 Penfield Drive
Montreal
Quebec H3A 1A9
Canada.

Italian Cultural Institute
496 Huron Street
Toronto
Canada.

Italian Cultural Institute
208-1200 Burrard Street
Vancouver B6Z 2CT
Canada.

Italian Consulates and Embassies

Italian Consulate General
38 Eaton Place
London SW1X 8AN.
UK
Tel: (071) 235 9371.

Italian Embassy
14 Three Kings Yard
London W1
UK
Tel: (071) 629 8200.

Italian Consulate
6 Melville Crescent
Edinburgh
UK.

Italian Consulate
111 Piccadilly
Manchester
UK.

Italian Vice-Consulate
23 Allhallows
Bedford
UK.

Italian Embassy
63 Northumberland Road
Dublin
Eire.

Italian Embassy
275 Slater Street
11th Floor
Ottawa KIP 5H9
Canada.

Italian Embassy
1601 Fuller Street NW
Washington DC 20009
USA.

Italian State Tourism Offices

Italian State Tourist Office
1 Princes Street
London W1R 8AY
UK
Tel: (071) 408 1254.

Italian State Tourist Office
47 Merrion Square
Dublin
Eire.

Italian State Tourism Office
3M9
1 Place Ville Marie
Suite 1914
Montreal
Quebec HEB
Canada.

Italian State Tourist Office
  630 Fifth Avenue
  Suite 1565
  New York
  NY10111
  USA.

Italian Trade Institutes

Italian Trade Centre (ICE)
  37 Sackville Street
  London W1X 2DQ
  UK
  Tel: (071) 734 2412.

Italian Chamber of Commerce
  Room 418-427 Walmar House
  296 Regent Street
  London W1R 5HB
  UK
  Tel: (071) 637 3153.

Italian Institute for Foreign Trade
  16 St Stephen's Green
  Dublin
  Eire.

Other useful addresses

The Royal Scottish Automobile
  Club
  11 Blythwood Square
  Glasgow G2 4AG
  UK.

Royal Automobile Club
  PO Box 100
  RAC House
  Landsdowne Road
  Croydon CR9 2JA
  UK.

Automobile Association
  Fanum House
  PO Box 51
  Basingstoke
  Hants RG21 2BH
  Tel: (0256) 469777.

Department of Social Security
  Overseas Branch
  Newcastle Upon Tyne
  NE98 1YX
  UK.

Animal Health Division 1B
  Government Buildings
  Hook Rise South
  Kingston By-Pass
  Surbiton
  Surrey KT6 7NF
  UK.

USEFUL ADDRESSES IN ITALY

Foreign Consulates and Embassies

British Embassy
  Via XX Settembre 80/A
  Rome
  Tel: (06) 4755441.

British Consulate
  Accademia
  Dorsoduro 1051
  Venice
  Tel: (041) 5227207/5227408.

British Consulate
  Via San Lucifero 87
  Cagliari
  Tel: (070) 662750.

British Consulate
Palazzo Castelbarco
Lungarno Corsini 2
Florence
Tel: (055) 284133.

British Consulate
Via XII Ottobre 2
Genoa
Tel: (010) 564833.

British Consulate
Via San Paolo 7
Milan
Tel: (02) 803442.

British Consulate
Via Francesco Crispi 122
Naples
Tel: (081) 663511.

British Consulate
Via delle Ville 15
Trieste
Tel: (040) 302884.

Canadian Embassy
Via G. B. de Rossi 27
Rome
Tel: (06) 4881851.

Irish Embassy
Largo del Nazareno 3
Rome
Tel: (06) 6782541.

USA Embassy
Via Vittorio Veneto 119/A
Rome
Tel: (06) 46741.

British Council
Via IV Fontane 20
Rome.

Ministries

Ministero della Pubblica
Istruzione
(Ministry of Public Education)
Viale Trastevere 76
Rome.

Ministero degli Affari Esteri
(Ministry of Foreign Affairs)
Ufficio IX
Piazzale della Farnesina
Rome.

Youth Information Centres

Informagiovani
Via Galimberti 2/a
Alessandria
Tel: (0131) 223366.

Informagiovani
Via Paleocapa 2
Bergamo
Tel: (035) 238187.

Centro Informazione e
Orientamento Professionale
Via Zamboni 8
Bologna
Tel: (051) 218328.

Centro Informazione Giovani
Piazza Vittoria 5
Brescia
Tel: (030) 2983505.

Centro Informagiovani
Piazza Dante 4
Caserta
Tel: (0832) 322822.

Servizio Informagiovani
Vicolo Santa Maria Maggiore 1
Florence
Tel: (055) 218310.

Centro Incontro
Via Pisana 578
Florence
Tel: (055) 713320.

Informagiovani
Via Goldoni 83
Livorno
Tel: (586) 50586.

Osmeg-Informshop
Via Vivaio 1
Milan
Tel: (02) 77402827.

Lombardia Lavoro
Via Ponchielli 24
Milan
Tel: (02) 29404675.

Centro Informazione Giovani
Via Scudari 8
Modena
Tel: (059) 206705.

Centro Informazioni
Documentazione Giovani
Corso Cavallotti 20
Novara
Tel: (0321) 23146.

Informagiovani
Vicolo Ponte Molino 7
Padua
Tel: (049) 654328.

Informagiovani
Via Oberdan 57
Pisa
Tel: (050) 595315.

Centro Informagiovani
Via del Can Bianco
Pistoia
Tel: (0573) 32928.

Centro Informagiovani
Via Mazzini 8
Ravenna.

Progetto Giovani
Via Mentana 9
Rimini
Tel: (0541) 24142.

National Secretariat
Coordinamento Nazionale
Sistema Informativo Giovanile
Via Palermo 28
Rome
Tel: (06) 4818089.

Informagiovani
Via G. Castano 29/31
Rome
Tel: (06) 2002635.

Informagiovani
Via Assarotti 2
Turin
Tel: (011) 57653572.

Servizio Orientamento
  Informagiovani
  Piazza Giovane Italia 6
  Varese
  Tel: (0322) 241565.

Centro Informagiovani
  Corso Portoni Borsari 17
  Verona
  Tel: (045) 597815.

Informagiovani Comune de
  Vicenza
  Contra San Tommaso 7
  Vicenza
  Tel: (0444) 228875.

Other useful addresses

Automobile Club Italiano
  Via Marsala 8
  Rome
  Tel: (06) 4212.

ABBREVIATIONS OF PROVINCES

The following is an alphabetical list of the abbreviations that are used for each of Italy's 95 provinces. You will see the abbreviations appear as the first two letters on car registration plates, in post codes and in official documents.

AG	Agrigento
AL	Alessandria
AN	Ancona
AO	Aosta
AP	Ascoli Piceno
AQ	Aquila
AR	Arezzo
AT	Asti
AV	Avellino
BA	Bari
BG	Bergamo
BL	Belluno
BN	Benevento
BO	Bologna
BR	Brindisi
BS	Brescia
BZ	Bolzano
CA	Cagliari
CB	Campobasso
CE	Caserta
CH	Chieti
CL	Caltanisetta
CN	Cuneo
CO	Como
CR	Cremona
CS	Cosenza
CT	Catania
CZ	Catanzaro
EN	Enna
FE	Ferrara
FG	Foggia
FI	Firenze
FO	Forli
FR	Frosinone
GE	Genova
GO	Gorizia
GR	Grosseto
IM	Imperia
IS	Isernia
LE	Lecce
LI	Livorno
LT	Latina
LU	Lucca
MC	Macerata
ME	Messina
MI	Milano
MN	Mantova

MO	Modena	UD	Udine
MS	Massa Carrara	VA	Varese
MT	Matera	VC	Vercelli
NA	Napoli	VE	Venezia
NO	Novara	VI	Vicenza
NU	Nuoro	VR	Verona
OR	Oristano	VT	Viterbo
PA	Palermo		
PC	Piacenza		
PD	Padova		
PE	Pescara		
PG	Perugia		
PI	Pisa		
PN	Pordenone		
PR	Parma		
PS	Pesaro		
PT	Pistoia		
PV	Pavia		
PZ	Potenza		
RA	Ravenna		
RC	Reggio Calabria		
RE	Reggio Emilia		
RG	Ragusa		
RI	Rieti		
RO	Rovigo		
ROMA	Roma		
SA	Salerno		
SI	Siena		
SO	Sondrio		
SP	Spezia		
SR	Siracusa		
SS	Sassari		
SV	Savona		
TA	Taranto		
TE	Teramo		
TN	Trento		
TO	Torino		
TP	Trapani		
TR	Terni		
TS	Trieste		
TV	Treviso		

ALPHABET BY NAMES

The following alphabetical list is used by all Italians to spell out words, especially over the telephone.

A Ancona
B Bologna
C Como
D Domodossola
E Empoli
F Firenze
G Genova
H Hotel
I Imola
K Kursaal
L Livorno
M Milano
N Napoli
O Otranto
P Padova
Q Quarto
R Roma
S Savona
T Torino
U Udine
V Venezia
W Washington
X Ics
Y York or Yacht
Z Zara

SOME FAMOUS ITALIANS TO KNOW

National leaders

Giuseppe Mazzini (1805-1872). The father of unified Italy.

Giuseppe Garibaldi (1808-1882). National hero and protagonist in unification of Italy.

Benito Mussolini (1883-1945). Fascist leader and founder of fascist party in 1921.

Medici, Cosimo the Elder (1389-1464). First Medici ruler.

Medici, Lorenzo the Magnificent (1449-1492). Medici ruler known for his patronage of the arts.

Camillo de Cavour (1810-1861). Diplomat central to the unification of Italy.

Writers, playwrights, poets

Luigi Pirandello (1867-1936). Writer and playwright of *6 Characters in Search of an Author*.

Alighieri Dante (1265-1321). Florentine poet, widely known for the *Divine Comedy*.

Francesco Petrarch (1304-1374). Poet who has lent his name to literary term 'petrarchism'.

Giovanni Boccaccio (1313-1375). Writer whose best known works include *The Decameron*.

Niccolo Macchiavelli (1469-1527). Wrote *The Prince*, known as the handbook for despots.

Benvenuto Cellini (1500-1571). Writer, provided a vivid record of 16th century life.

Alberto Moravia (born 1907). Pseudonym of the writer Alberto Pincherle.

Primo Levi (1919-1987). Writer who wrote of his experience of a Nazi war camp.

Gabriele d'Annunzio (1863-1938). Poet known for his decadent lifestyle and bizarre poetry.

Carlo Levi (1902-1975). Writer and painter, author of *Christ Stopped at Eboli*.

Painters, sculptors

Sandro Botticelli (1444-1510). Influential 15th century Florentine painter.

Buonarroti Michelangelo (1475-1564). Painted, among many outstanding works, the Sistine Chapel.

Leonardo da Vinci (1452-1519). Known as the Renaissance Universal Man.

Sanzio Rafaello (Raphael) (1483-1520). One of the great creators of the Renaissance.

Vecellio Tiziano (Titian) (1487/90-1576). Important Venetian painter.

Gianlorenzo Bernini (1598-1680). Tuscan sculptor.

Giorgio Vasari (1511-1574). Primarily an art historian although also painted and practised architecture.

Duccio di Buoninsegna (1255/60-1315/18). Master Sienese painter.

Donatello (c1386-1466). Greatest sculptor in Florence before Michelangelo.

Giovanni Cimabue (c1240-1302). Artist often associated with Giotto.

Fra Angelico (1387-1455). Painter and Domenican friar.

Piero della Francesca (1410-1492). One of best-loved painters of 15th century.

Jacopo Tintoretto (1518-1594). Venetian Mannerist painter.

Andrea Palladio (1508-1580). Influential Italian architect.

Paolo Veronese (1528-1588). Verona artist, influenced by Titian.

Antonio Canaletto (1697-1768). Famous for paintings of Venice views.

Amedeo Modigliani (1884-1920). Greatest Italian painter of 20th century.

Giorgio Dechirico (1888-1978). Quasi surrealist painter.

Michelangelo Merisi Caravaggio (1573-1610). Painter of realist style.

Andrea Mantegna (1410-1506). Painter, influenced by Donatello.

Antonio Correggio (1489-1534). Worked as a painter in Parma; his style anticipated the Baroque.

Scientists

Galilei Galileo (1564-1642). Scientist and mathematician who evolved theories on gravity and the pendulum.

Guglielmo Marconi (1874-1937). Invented the first radio.

Luigi Galvani (1737-1798). Anatomist, discovered electricity in animals.

Enrico Fermi (1901- 1954). Made first sustained nuclear reaction.

Alessandro Volta (1747-1827). Physicist, discovered the electrical volt.

Evangelista Torricelli (1608-1647). Mathematician and physicist; invented the mercury barometer.

Religious figures

St Francis of Assisi (1181-1226). Founder of the Franciscan Order.

St Anthony of Padua (1195-1231). Born in Portugal but preached and died in Padua.

St Benedict (c480-547). Father of western monasticism.

St Bernardine of Siena (1380-1444). Influential leader in Franciscan movement.

St Bona of Pisa (1156-1207). Patron saint of travellers.

St Callistus the First (died 222). Pope and martyr.

St Catherine of Siena. (c1347-1380). Now considered a doctor of the church.

St Celestine the First (died 432). Bishop of Rome in 422.

St Celestine the Fifth (1214-1296). 80 year old hermit elected pope, died after 10 months.

St Charles Borromeo (1538-1584). Bishop and cardinal, of aristocratic descent.

St Clare of Assisi (1194-1253). Founded order of Poor Clares in association with St Francis.

St Clement the First (died end of 1st century). First of apostolic fathers, symbol is the anchor.

St Francis Borgia (1510-1572). Jesuit and great grandson of ill-reputed Pope Alexander VI.

St Ambrose (334-397). One of the great Latin doctors of the church.

St Gregory the Great (540-604). First and greatest of 16 popes of same name.

St Gregory the Seventh (1020-1085). Heralded an era of ecclesiastical reform.

St Januarius (died 305?). A phial of this saint's blood is kept in the cathedral at Naples and is said to liquefy at auspicious moments.

St Lawrence (died 258). Martyred by being grilled on a grid.

St Leo the Great (died 461). Bishop of Rome, influential in early history of papacy.

St Martin the First (died 655). Pope and martyr.

St Paul of the Cross (1694-1775). Founded order of Passionists devoted to Saviour's cross and Passion.

St Peter Orseolo (928-987). Doge of Venice.

St Pius the Fifth (1504-1572). Pope and friar of the Domenican order.

St Pius the Tenth (1835-1914). Pope while state and church were separated in France.

St Scholastica (c480-543). Sister of St Benedict.

St Silvester the First (died 335). Pope and first non-martyr to be made a saint.

St Thomas Aquinas (1225-1274). Theologian and doctor of the church.

St Valentine (date unknown). Feast day 14th February.

Musicians

Antonio Vivaldi (1676-1741). Composer and musician; among his best known works is the *Four Seasons*.

Vincenzo Bellini (1801-1835). Composer of opera.

Gaetano Donizetti (1797-1848). Composed more than sixty operas.

Gioacchino Rossini (1792-1868). Composed many operas including the *Barber of Seville*.

Giuseppe Verdi (1813-1901). Composer of operas including *Rigoletto, La Traviata, Aida*.

Nicolo Paganini (1782-1840). Violinist and composer.

Alessandro Scarlatti (1660-1725). Composed Neopolitan operas popular in 18th century.

Giacomo Puccini (1858-1924). Composed operas including *La Bohème, Tosca, Madame Butterfly*.

Claudio Monteverdi (1567-1924). Composed some of earliest major operatic works.

Luciano Pavarotti (born 1936). Tenor, eminent in the world of opera.

Arturo Toscanini (1867-1957). Conductor of concerts and operas.

Antonio Stradivari (1645-1737). One of family of violin makers in Cremona.

Film-makers

Luchino Visconti (1906-1976). Neo-realist film-maker.

Roberto Rossellini (1906-1977). Made many films starring Ingrid Bergman.

Federico Fellini (1920-). Amalgamated neo-realist ideals.

Michelangelo Antonioni (1912-). Neo-realist film-maker.

Francesco Rosi (1922-) Often worked with Visconti.

Pier Paolo Pasolini (1922-1975). Film-maker and writer.

Franco Zeffirelli (1923-). Amongst most recent films was *Who's Afraid of Virginia Woolf*.

Explorers

Marco Polo (1254-1324). Travelled across Asia to Peking.

Cristoforo Colombo (1447-1506). Credited with the discovery of America.

Education

Maria Montessori (1870-1952). Created the Montessori method of education.

Glossary

PASSPORTS, VISAS AND PERMITS

certificato di equipollenza	certificate of academic equivalence
certificato residenza	residence permit
cittadino	nationality
codice fiscale	fiscal code number
domicilio	address
firma	signature
giorno	day
nome, cognome	forename, surname
passaporto	passport
permesso di soggiorno	permit to stay
scopo lavorativo	for the purpose of work
scopo residenza	for the purpose of residence
sottoscritto	undersigned
Ufficio Anagrafe	Municipal Registry Office
Ufficio Collocamento	Italian Employment Office
Ufficio Imposte Dirette	Provincial Tax Office
Ufficio Stranieri	Foreign Department
valido (fino al)	valid (until)

TRAVEL

abbonamento	season ticket
Automobile Club d'Italia (ACI)	Italian Automobile Club
autostrada	motorway
benzina normale/super	regular/super grade petrol
biglietto, biglietti, biglietteria	ticket, tickets/ticket office

Carta Verde	Youth Rail Card
chilometrico	ticket allowing 3,000km free rail travel
conducento anonimo	unnamed driver
corso	main street, boulevard
entrata	entrance
Ferrovie Statale	State Railway System
mezza pensione	half board
Ministero del Trasporto	Ministry of Transport
numero targa	number plate
incrocio	crossroads
lavori in corso	road works ahead
passaggio a livello	level crossing
pensione	boarding houses
pericolo	danger
rallentare	slow down
Scheda tecnica	Schedule of technical data on a vehicle
senso vietato	no entry
senso unico	one way
sosta autorizzato	parking permitted at certain times
sosta vietato	no parking
strada (privata)	road (private)
uscita	exit
verde	lead-free petrol
verde verde	higher octane lead-free petrol
Viacard	Motorway toll card
zona blu	parking within blue lines only
zona disco	parking within restricted time
zona rimozione	no parking: cars will be towed away
zona tutelato	no parking either side of road
vietato ingresso	no entry
affitasi/da affitare	to rent
bollo	chit or state stamp
bonus/malus	insurance policy based on no claims bonuses
buste	payslips
camera di commercio	chamber of commerce
commercialista	book-keeper, accountant

denuncia	statement; income tax return
franchigia	insurance policy with an excess limit
gettone	token (eg for pay phones)
imposte	tax
ricevuta fiscale	receipt
Scala mobili	Wage indexation
tangenti	kick-backs, bribes
Ufficio Imposte Dirette	Provincial Tax Office

GENERAL

agenzia	agent, agency
alimentari	grocery stores
antiquario	antique shop
calzolaio	shoe repairer
Carta Si	an Italian Credit Card
cartolibreria	bookshop
casa del formaggio	cheese shop
casa di pasta	pasta shop
comune, municipio	town hall
denuncia	legal/police statement
elenchi telefonici	telephone directories
enoteca	wine merchant
fai da te	DIY
farmacia	chemist
ferramenta	hardware store
francobolli	postage stamp
gabinetti	WC
gelateria	ice cream shop
macelleria	butchers shop
mercato	market
omertá	Mafia law of silence
paneficio/panetteria	bakery
parrucchiere	hairdresser
passeggiata	evening stroll or promenade
pescheria	fishmonger
profumeria	perfumery
saldi	sales
signore, signori	ladies, gentlemen

supermercato	supermarket
tabacchi	tobacconists
tintoria	drycleaner
toiletta	WC
Tribunale	Magistrates Court
Ufficio Postale	Post Office
Vigili Urbani	Town Police

Further Reading

GENERAL

Getting It Right in Italy: A Manual for the 1990s, William Ward (Bloomsbury, 1990).
How to Get a Job in Europe, Mark Hempshell (How To Books, 1992).
How to Retire Abroad, Roger Jones (How To Books, 1993).
Italy 1993 (Fodor Gold Guide Series, 1992).
Welcome to Italy: A Guide for Young People (Intercultura, Rome)
Working Abroad: Essential Financial Planning for Expatriates and their Employers, Jonathan Golding (International Venture Handbooks, Plymbridge Distributors, Plymouth).

PROPERTY

Doing Business in Italy, Dalbert Hallenstein (BBC Books, 1991).
Gardens of the Italian Villas, Marcella Agnelli (Weidenfeld & Nicolson, 1987).
How to Rent & Buy Property in Italy, Amanda Hinton (How To Books, 1993).
Italian Living Design: Three Decades of Interiors, Giuseppi Raimondi (Taurus Parke, 1990). Translated from the Italian.
Italian Splendour: Palaces, Castles & Villas, Jack Basehart (Rizzoli, 1990).
Italy: Practical Commercial Law, Roberto Barbalich (Longman, 1991).
Setting Up in Italy, Sebastian O'Kelly (Merehurst Press, 1990).
Urban Land and Property Markets in Italy, Gastone Ave (UCLP, 1993).
Your Home in Italy, F. Maxwell (Longman Professional, 1989).

REGIONAL GUIDES

Baedeker's Italy (Automobile Association, 1993).

Italian Journeys, Jonathan Keates (Picador, 1992).
Italy: Insight Guides Series (APA Publications, 1992).
Italy: Off the Beaten Track Series, Richard Sale (Moorland, 1993).
Italy: The Hill Towns, James Bentley (George Philip, 1990).
Italy by Train, Tim Jepson (Hodder & Stoughton, 1993).
Lombardy: The Italian Lakes, John Flower (Philip, 1990).
Milan, Richard Sale (Crowood, 1991).
A Place in Italy, Simon Mawer (Sinclair-Stevenson, 1992).
Southern Italy: A Traveller's Guide, Paul Holberton (Murray, 1992).
Southern Italy: From Rome to Calabria, Paul Blanchard (Blue Guides, 1990).
Tuscany, Umbria and the Marches, Michael Pauls & Dana Facaros (Cadogan, 1992).
Umbria: Maps and Plans, Alta Macadam (Blue Guides, 1993).

FOOD AND WINE

The Best of Italy: A Cook Book, edited by Evie Righter (Harper Collins, 1993).
Classic Italian Cook Book, Marcella Hazan (Papermacs, 1988).
From an Italian Garden: Traditional Fruit and Vegetable Recipes from Italy, Judith Barrett (Michael Joseph, 1993).
Gourmet's Companion: Italian Menu Guide and Translator, Bernard Rivkin (Wiley, 1991).
Hamlyn All Colour Italian Cook Book (Hamlym All Colour Cookery Series, 1993).
Invitation to Italian Cooking, Antonio Carluccio (Pavilion Books, 1991).
Italian Country Cooking, Anne Willan (Dorling Kindersley, 1993).
Italian Wines, Phillip Dallas (Faber, 1989).
Mitchell Beazley Guide to Italian Wines, Burton Anderson (Mitchell Beazley, 1992).
Pocket Guide to Italian Food and Wine, Spike & Charmian Hughes (Carbery Press, 1992).
Recipes from an Italian Farmhouse, Valentina Harris (Conran Octopus, 1993).
Second Classic Italian Cook Book, Marcella Hazan (Papermacs, 1990).
Secrets from an Italian Kitchen, Anna del Conte (Corgi, 1993).
Valentina Harris's Italian Cookery Course, Valentina Harris (BBC Books, 1992).
Wine Atlans of Italy, Burton Anderson (Mitchell Beazley, 1990).
Wine Roads of Italy, Marc & Kim Millon (Fontana, 1992).

CITY GUIDES

Florence
Everyman's Guide to Florence (Everyman's Library, 1993).
Florence, Alta Macadam (Blue Guides: A & C Black, 1991).
Florence: A Literary Companion, Francis King (Murray, 1991).
Florence from the Air, Mario Sabbieti (Weidenfeld & Nicolson, 1990).
Florence and Tuscany, Sheila Hale (Mitchell Beazley, 1992).

Rome
Rome, Anthony Pereira & Nick Skidmore (Mitchell Meazley, 1992).
Rome: Holy Cities Series, Saviour Pirotta (Evans Brothers, 1992).
Rome: Architecture, History and Art, James Bentley (George Philip, 1991).

Venice
Everyman's Guide to Venice (Everyman's Library, 1993).
Venice, Dorothy Bohm (Thames & Hudson, 1992).
Venice: Lascelles City Guides (Lascelles, 1992).
Venice: A Literary Companion, Ian Littlewood (Murray, 1991).
Venice: The Four Seasons, Lisa St Aubin de Teran (Pavilion Books, 1992).
Venice and the Veneto, James Bentley (Aurum, 1992).
Venice Desired, Tony Tanner (Blackwell, 1992).
Venicewalks, Charles Carner & Alessandro Giannatasio (Robson, 1991).

ITALIAN CULTURE

Art and Architecture
Art and Architecture in Italy 1250-1400, John White (Yale University Press, 1993).
Architecture of the Italian Renaissance, Peter Murray (Thames & Hudson, 1969).
History of Italian Renaissance Art, Frederick Hartt (Thames & Hudson, 1988).
Italian Renaissance Painting, Keith Roberts (Phaidon, 1993).
Italian Renaissance Sculpture: World of Art Series, Roberta Olson (Thames & Hudson, 1992).
Painting in Italy, S.J. Freeberg (Yale University Press Pelican History of Art Series, 1993).

Cinema

Italian Cinema: From Neorealism to the Present, Petre Bondanella (Continuum USA, 1991).

Italian Films, Robin Buss (Batsford, 1990).

Design

Italian Modern: A Design Heritage, Giovanni Albera & Nicolas Monti (Rizzolini, 1989).

New Italian Design, Nally Bellati (Rizzoli, 1990).

History

A Traveller's History of Italy, Valerio Lintner (Windrush, 1989).

The Florentine Renaissance, Vincent Cronin (Pimlico, 1992).

The Penguin Book of the Renaissance, J.H. Plumb (Penguin, 1964, reprinted 1991).

Italy: A Short History, Harry Hearder (Cambridge University Press, 1990).

History of the Italian People, Giuliano Procacci (Penguin, 1991).

Literature

Italian Short Stories (No. 1), R. Trevelyan (Penguin, 1965).

Italian Short Stories (No. 2), D. Vittorini (Penguin, 1972).

Italian Stories in English and Italian, Robert Hall (Dover, 1990).

Music

Golden Century of Italian Opera from Rossini to Puccini, William Weaver (Thames & Hudson, 1988).

Masters of Italian Opera, Philip Gossett (Papermacs, 1983).

Index

Other books in this series

How to Live & Work in Spain
Robert A C Richards

Long popular with Britons for holidays and retirement, Spain is now an increasingly important focus for commercial life. Written by a British expatriate who has lived and worked in Spain for more than 25 years, this new book provides a user-friendly guide for everyone planning to live in Spain on a temporary or permanent basis, whether for business, professional purposes, study, leisure or retirement. Written with considerable gusto, the book gives a fascinating warts'n'all account of Spain's variegated lifestyles and how to cope. 'As well as the sort of information one might expect eg work permits, visas, property buying and financial matters, there is so much additional information on health care, travel, holidays, history, geography etc that I feel it would be a good read for the more casual visitor. . . The information is presented in an orderly and interesting way.' *Phoenix/Association of Graduate Careers Advisory Services.*

160pp illus. 1 85703 011 7

How to Live & Work in Belgium
Marvina Shilling

Researched and written by a specialist on Belgian affairs, this is a complete manual of essential information on Belgium from entering the country to taking up residence, coping with the language, living in Brussels, Antwerp and other major cities, understanding the business, official and legal environment, the cost of living and other vital facts and advice for executives, officials, technicians, students, teachers and others. 'Interesting, easy to read and full of fascinating information . . . Gives a succinct and enlightening explanation for the use of both the French and Dutch language and the political tensions engendered by this language split.' *Phoenix/Association of Graduate Careers Advisory Services.* 'A crisp and clear resumé. . . If companion volumes are on a similar par, a European collection would be particularly appropriate.' *Newscheck/Careers Service Bulletin.*

139pp illus. 1 85703 053 2.

How to Live & Work in Portugal
Sue Tyson-Ward

A new guide for short and longstay visitors to one of Europe's oldest, most charming and best-value countries: covers entry requirements, finding a place to stay, employment, doing business, getting around, health, education and more.

144pp illus. 1 85703 085 0.

How to Live & Work in Germany
Nessa Loewenthal

West and East Germany formally became a single nation in October 1990. The real work of unification is likely to take many years, but this process — added to the ultimate potential for economic and cultural growth — makes this an exciting time to live in Germany. Whether you are planning to relocate for three months or three years, this is the book for you. It covers such practical topics as entry requirements, transportation, money matters, housing, schools, insurance and much besides. It also includes valuable pointers to German values, customs, business practices and etiquette to help you make the most of your stay. Nessa Loewenthal is Director of Trans Cultural Services, and a consultant specialising in intercultural briefing. 'Detailed help is given on how to find work in Germany including . . . a comprehensive list of organisations which offer the chance to combine the experience of living in Germany with a useful activity.' *Phoenix/Association of Graduate Careers Advisory Services.*

142pp illus. 1 85703 006 0.

How to Get a Job in Europe
Mark Hempshell

Europe's rise as the world's leading economic unit has made it *the* place to get a job. This book is the first to set out exactly what opportunities exist in Europe. It contains step-by-step guidance on how to find the vacancies, how to apply, and how to understand and adapt to the cultural and legal framework. Packed throughout with key contacts, sample documents and much hard-to-find information, this book will be an absolutely essential starting point for everyone job-hunting in Europe, whether as a school or college leaver, graduate trainee, technician or professional — and indeed anyone wanting to live and work as a European whether for just a summer vacation or on a more permanent basis. Mark Hempshell is a freelance writer who specialises in writing on overseas employment. 'Well written, clear and interesting — this is a very useful book and would be a valuable addition to any careers library.' *Phoenix/Association of Graduate Careers Advisory Services.*

208pp illus. 1 85703 060 5.

How to Get a Job Abroad
Roger Jones

This top-selling title is essential for everyone planning to spend a period abroad. It contains a big reference section of medium and long-term job opportunities and possibilities, arranged by region and country of the world, and by profession/occupation. There are more than 130 pages of specific contacts and leads, giving literally hundreds of addresses and much hard-to-find information. There is a classified guide to overseas recruitment agencies, and even a multi-lingual guide to writing application letters. 'A fine book for anyone considering even a temporary overseas job.' *The Evening Star.* 'A highly informative and well researched book. . . containing lots of hard information and a first class reference section. . . A superb buy.' *The Escape Committee Newsletter.* 'A valuable addition to any careers library.' *Phoenix (Association of Graduate Careers Advisory Services).* 'An excellent addition to any careers library . . . Compact and realistic. . . There is a wide range of reference addresses covering employment agencies, specialist newspapers, a comprehensive booklist and helpful addresses . . . All readers, whether careers officers, young adults or more mature adults, will find use for this book.' *Newscheck/Careers Services Bulletin.*

288pp illus. 1 85703 003 6. Second Edition

How to Get a Job in America
Roger Jones BA(Hons) DipEd DPA

Millions of people around the world dream of landing a job in the States, despite the strict immigration controls now in force. This book helps you to turn your dream into reality by explaining the work possibilities open to non-US citizens. Drawing on the experience of individuals, companies and recruitment agencies Roger Jones reveals the range of jobs available, the locations, pay and conditions, and how to get hired. The book includes the latest on immigration procedures following the 1990 US Immigration Act. 'Excellent . . . provides you with every scrap of information you'll need when going to the USA to work, from the sort of lifestyle you can expect to job contacts and prospective salaries.' *Going USA.* 'Very good value for money.' *The School Librarian.* 'For young people considering a US exchange or summer employment the section on vacation jobs is particularly worthwhile.' *Newscheck/COIC.*

224pp illus. 1 85703 047 8.

How to Get a Job in Australia
Nick Vandome

With ever-increasing competition for entry into Australia and its employment market it is essential for migrant job-hunters to arm themselves with as much practical and relevant information as possible. This handbook provides a complete step-by-step guide to all aspects of job-finding in Australia, for both casual and permanent employment. Where to look for work, what pay and conditions to expect, and the current economic climate is explained alongside key information about tax, contracts, your rights at work and the Australian philosophy of employment; all you need to know to earn your Aussie dollars. Nick Vandome has himself worked and travelled extensively in Australia. He has written articles for several Australian publications including *The Melbourne Age*, and is author of **How to Spend a Year Abroad** in this series. 'One book we strongly recommend.' *Australian News*. 'Very good value indeed.' *Newscheck/COIC*, 'Indispensable.' *TNT Magazine*.

176pp illus. 1 85703 048 6.

How to Get a Job in France
Mark Hempshell

This is the first book which sets out clearly how to get a job in France, whether for example in catering, tourism, teaching, computing, retailing, or other craft, industry, business or profession. We are all today not only part of a national economy, but a European — and even global — marketplace; and for those willing to surmount cultural and language barriers, the rewards in standard and quality of life can be considerable. This most informative book is packed with helpful information and guidance on every aspect of the French employment scene and will be a valuable resource for everyone concerned with the growing subject of international employment. Mark Hempshell is a specialist researcher and author on the European employment scene. 'Makes a bold attack on the subject and succeeds in covering a lot of important issues.' *French Property News*.

159pp illus. 1 85703 081 8.

How to Rent & Buy Property in France
Clive Kristen

Interest in French property has never been greater. Prices are lower than in the UK, and the French climate and culture are powerful incentives to renters and buyers. Honest independent advice, however, is hard to come by. If you are thinking about buying or renting a second home, or moving to France to work or retire, this practical book will guide you step-by-step through the pitfalls of loans, contracts, and even setting up a profitable gîte business. It covers: your renting/buying decision, the options, regions, rentals and timeshares, relocating to France, banking, taxation, wills, mortgages, loans, insurance, the purchase process, building or buying a property under construction, running your own gîte business, and more. Complete with specimen forms and documents. Clive Kristen MEd is an experienced teacher and lecturer with a special interest in France and the French legal system, and has full personal experience of buying and renting property in France.

160pp illus. 1 85703 072 9.

How to Rent & Buy Property in Italy
Amanda Hinton

Provides a very practical and thorough treatment of the subject, and includes helpful checklists, glossaries of key terms, and examples of all the documents and forms you are likely to come across. Written by a UK citizen resident in Italy.

160pp illus. 1 85703 099 0.